THE ART OF THE SALES MEETING

THE ART OF THE

SALES

MEETING

**Performance Techniques for
CONFIDENCE AND RESULTS**

CHRIS PRANGLEY

Bestselling author of *THE TECH SALES WARRIOR*

LIONCREST
PUBLISHING

THE ART OF THE SALES MEETING

Performance Techniques for Confidence and Results

FIRST EDITION

ISBN 978-1-5445-3830-3 Hardcover
      978-1-5445-3828-0 Paperback
      978-1-5445-3829-7 Ebook

To my teachers and coaches

for opening my eyes to what I couldn't see

and pushing me past what I could.

CONTENTS

INTRODUCTION 1

CHAPTER 1
THE BLANK PAGE 15

CHAPTER 2
KNOWING YOUR "PART" 29

CHAPTER 3
THE LAB 51
Crafting and Practicing Your Pitch

CHAPTER 4
PREPARING FOR THE STAGE 87

CHAPTER 5
WHAT TO DO IN THE SPOTLIGHT 101

CHAPTER 6
THE MAGIC OF DISCOVERY 125

CHAPTER 7

PRICING: A COMMON
PERFORMANCE PITFALL 145

CHAPTER 8

DEPARTING IN STYLE 167

CHAPTER 9

FOLLOWING UP 185

CHAPTER 10

DIRECTOR'S NOTES 203

CONCLUSION 221

ACKNOWLEDGMENTS 231

ABOUT THE AUTHOR 235

INTRODUCTION

I could have been Superman, but Henry Cavill turned out to be my kryptonite, and he got to fly in the Man of Steel movie instead of me.

I almost stood next to Tom Cruise in a scene from the Steven Spielberg movie *Minority Report*—but I was too tall.

Trekkie chat boards claimed I was going to be the next Captain Kirk in the Star Trek Series, but Chris Pine beamed me to it.

And I came heartbreakingly close to landing a role on the legendary HBO series *The Sopranos*, but ultimately was rejected because of my pronunciation of a tiny two-letter word.

Those are a few frustrating snapshots from my first career as an actor, but don't get me wrong—I am not looking for anyone to throw me a pity party. For one thing, I hate pity parties because failure always leads to growth if you know to look for it. And for another, there were great times, too.

I landed a co-star role on the mega-popular CBS series *Criminal Minds*. I did work and training with well-known improv groups like Upright Citizens Brigade, The Groundlings, and Second City Chicago. There were national TV commercials, soap opera roles, and lots of other stuff that was a ton of fun. There was a pilot with Ashton Kutcher's Co. Katalyst Media and theater roles.

I did dozens of print campaigns, including one for Axe Body Spray, where they plastered me in major magazines, billboards, and on multiple stories of skyscrapers in every major city in the United States.

I also got to train and learn from some of the top acting teachers in the country. I wouldn't trade the experience for anything. By the end of my journey, I was fully confident to pick up any script and walk onto any studio lot with passion, not fear. I would willingly stand in my power in any audition room, even if the biggest directors, producers, writers, and casting directors in the world were staring right back at me.

Anything I was able to accomplish as an actor had everything to do with tools and training. The only reason I could embrace faceoffs against leading celebrities with competitive talents and tackle high-stress, make-or-break moments with purpose and ease was because of what I had learned in coaching, in classes, and in my experiences.

* * *

Let's pause here for just a second. Because maybe you're starting to think, "Hey, I bought a book about how to get better at sales meetings, and this guy is telling me about his time as an actor. What is going on?"

Fair question. I promise you this book will not be some lame attempt at a "humble brag" about my time as an actor. And it won't be some indulgent trip down memory lane. I wouldn't waste your time.

This book *is* all about how to master the art of the sales meeting. But what is interesting is this: when I left acting to begin my second career in tech sales, I discovered to my pleasant surprise, that I already had mastered many of the skills needed to run an excellent sales meeting. They were many of the same skills that I had learned through honing the craft of performance in my decade-plus of study and learning the craft of acting. And although it took me years to learn and harness these skills, I'm hoping this book will empower you to use my experience to learn these lessons quicker so you can achieve extraordinary success in your own sales meetings.

So how did I go from acting to tech sales and then discover the surprising overlap of skills between these two fields? Here's the super concise version of that story.

With my acting career, I eventually reached a crossroads. On the positive side, I felt good about some of the work I was able to do (and had a lot of fun doing it). Most of all, I loved it as a craft, and I got to study with some amazing people, well-known folks in the field who were truly experts. It was a true passion.

But there was a flip side. First, there were some significant student loans hanging over my head (think $100K+!). I also had my regular living expenses to pay, a dream to travel more, a bond to always take care of family, a desire to invest more, an interest in owning a home, and a hope of building my own family one day. Money tends to come in handy for all those things.

It's a common hazard of the acting profession to have a near-constant nagging feeling of financial instability. You feel great after booking a gig, but whether it pays $10,000 or $200,000, you still don't know when your next gig will arrive or how much it will pay. The career is a constant job interview filled with a near-daily sensation of chasing "it"—a feeling of "maybe" and "almost." But the craft behind acting is so intriguing that many find themselves fighting through the constant rejection, the lack of control over a career, and the rollercoaster of sometimes getting a role but often not. Add in the unstable money, no health insurance, and the often humbling nature of the job, and it can be tough to hang on just to get another taste of the magic.

Despite how great that magic could sometimes be, I eventually totaled up everything and decided it was time to take a different path. I entered the world of tech sales.

Fast forward. After several years in the sales game, I was offered a bit part in a scene with Kevin Spacey in the hit series on Netflix, *House of Cards*. I turned it down for a very important customer meeting. And that was the moment I knew I was all-in on my new life in tech sales.

One of the reasons I could commit to this career was because of what I had witnessed since I had made the jump to tech sales. When I started going to meetings, I saw that a lot of sales reps struggled mightily to connect with their prospects. There was a fundamental breakdown of what should have been the basics for running a sales meeting.

There was no research. Poor questions. Missed opportunities to link customer problems with the solution the rep could provide.

There was also too much anxiety. Many reps were tense and swallowed words. They did not control their body movement, lacked eye contact, and were sometimes less than presentable.

Worst of all, there was no precision in how they communicated. Reps would run on with words to the point of gibberish. There was no follow-up on something crucial the prospect shared. The passion and focus were lacking, and there was no sense of timing or purpose. Added all together, it was BORING! And as a consequence, sales suffered because these reps failed to close.

All this failure intrigued me because I felt sales did not have to be such a mystery. At the time I began witnessing this, I was a young cold caller (think TDR, BDR, SDR level), but my observations have held true all through my journey as I evolved from inside rep to commercial rep to enterprise rep to regional director to senior director and onto a VP role. It was the same challenges I was seeing all along.

The first huge challenge for a sales rep is, of course, prospecting. You have to have a viable and successful pipeline of leads, or you can't get anywhere. But once that is mastered, the biggest factor in success is the ability to run a meeting well.

Yet somehow, it's an area that firms and sales coaches spend the least amount of time training their people on. Tone, timing, clarity, active listening, rapport, preparation, inflection, and eye contact—all the keys to communication—have fallen by the wayside. Even the best sales trainings seem to overlook these skills.

If you look at the past decade, the science of sales and the measuring of its metrics have all taken giant leaps forward. There are fantastic marketing tools and research solutions. There are new advanced callers, better outsourcing, and terrific outreach software options.

But getting better at communication? Pretty much ignored. Ask yourself, how many failed meetings have you sat through?

Some think that advances in artificial intelligence (AI) will solve communication issues or at least greatly improve them. A piece of software tracking the speed of a meeting, watching the minutes you stay on a slide, or generically monitoring how much time you speak vs. your prospect may marginally help you in a general way. But anyone thinking that this type of software will become some kind of silver bullet is going to be disappointed.

The only thing that will solve this is learning to connect: human to human.

Let me take this back to the world of acting to illustrate. A successful director does not just instruct an actor to "cry here." Instead, a great director guides the actor by laying out the facts of the scene and then coaches the actor's imagination to respond with the proper emotion. It's about connection, not creating a cookie-cutter response.

In the same way, as a sales rep you need to connect with the "facts of the scene." What is your customer's pain? What is their deep why—the problem they need solved urgently? You need to use your passion and your communication skills to connect with them and coach them to the right solution, like the best directors do with actors.

This book's goal is to give you those kinds of skills, the ones I first learned as an actor that allowed me to transition to sales and find success relatively quickly.

Mastering the principles, strategies, and tactics behind successful sales meetings does not require an acting background, of course. But I do think my previous career has given me a unique angle of approach, one that can be useful to anyone who wants clear and practical ways to feel confident in meetings while improving your conversion rates.

The methods you will learn here have been road-tested, both by me and the tech salespeople I have mentored, and they work for anyone who puts in the time to practice and learn them. No special talent is required to find massive success in closing more sales. It's about understanding what works and then applying it.

And that should sound exciting to you because it means the only thing that can stop you from getting better is if you fail to implement what you learn here. The choice to get exponentially better in meetings and close more sales and drive your income way up is completely in your hands.

THIS IS NOT ABOUT BEING FAKE!

Before diving into more specifics about the tools themselves, I'd like to clarify a few things right off. When I talk about an actor's performance in relation to how you run a sales meeting, I am not saying I will teach you to "perform a meeting" like an actor performs on stage.

It's not about learning to create a performance; it is about using the same tools that make an actor successful to get better at sales meetings. A few quick examples:

- Great actors have to research their characters and spend a lot of rehearsal time preparing for their roles. A great tech salesperson has to research the company and the main players that will be in the meeting and then spend time preparing to be in the spotlight.
- Outstanding actors need to know how to stay focused in the moment, even when unexpected distractions happen from backstage or from the audience. Outstanding salespeople need to remain focused, present, and on point, if thrown off balance by an unexpected question or a presentation mistake.
- Top actors spend time after a performance breaking down what they did right and what they could have done better. Top salespeople review their meetings to recall what they got right and what they got wrong and how they can avoid repeating a mistake.

So again, none of this is about performing as an actor performs. It is about what can be learned from the craft of acting that can be transferred into the arena of sales to enormously improve your ability to master meetings, even ones that involve high-level executives and lots of pressure.

I also want to dispense with another idea that some may have about acting and sales. This book is not about being fake. Absolutely none of this book will teach you to be someone you are not or how to put on a show to fool prospective clients. (It is also wrong to think that an actor's job is to be "fake." That's a very superficial view of what leading actors do and is not an accurate description of what their real work or craft is about).

The stereotypical salesperson as a slick operator trying to trick people into buying is the viewpoint of an amateur or someone not aware of the power of a salesperson. Are there a few bad apples out there who think like this? Of course, just like there are a few bad folks in every industry. But I can tell you from experience that the overwhelming majority of the most successful people in sales know that they are there to solve problems for clients. Tricks, fakery, and "putting on a performance" have nothing to do with it. It's the same in acting: those that fake their way through a scene eventually fail, collapsing in the moment, and end up embarrassed.

So, if this isn't going to be about "putting on a show" or faking your way through meetings, what is it about?

WHAT THIS BOOK CAN DO FOR YOU—
AND WHAT IT CAN'T

Let's start with three things this book cannot do for you:

- It can't force you to implement what you learn. The desire and the work are going to have to come from you. That may sound obvious, but it is all too common for people to never implement what they learn. It's up to you to do your own "gut check" and ask yourself if you have the courage to up your game. And it will take some courage because...
- This book can't prevent you from getting bumps and bruises along the way. Setbacks and failures are an inevitable part of the road to mastery. This book will show you exactly what skills to develop, so you don't waste time working on the wrong things. And you'll get some great strategies for overcoming the fear of failure. But ultimately, only you can decide to push through inevitable setbacks and keep going.
- What you learn here will also not help you if you are not generating enough quality leads on a consistent basis. Being great in meetings isn't worth much if you aren't getting enough of them! (If you struggle in this area, I recommend starting with my first book, *The Tech Sales Warrior: Battle-Tested Strategies to Crush Quota*. Then

return to this book when you have your lead pipeline in a consistently healthy state.)

What this book CAN do for you is reveal the key fundamentals for becoming a true master of the art of the sales meeting. You will learn the performance techniques of actors that you can translate into confidence and results when it's time for you to command a room. You'll learn everything from the overarching concepts and strategies down to the nitty-gritty details and practical tips you need to be successful.

We'll start off the journey by laying the right foundation. Not only do you need to make sure your overall mental and physical health are solid, but you also should fully understand the mindset necessary to go from unsure in meetings to a confident, results-oriented salesperson in charge of the room.

Next, you'll learn how crucial research is to success. Just like actors have to have a script down cold and understand the motivations of their character, a master of meetings always goes in knowing their goal, having a strategy, and understanding the necessary background information about their potential customer.

Then you'll get a crash course on crafting and practicing a pitch, including the fifteen things you need to be mindful of when delivering a pitch. You'll also learn the extremely practical things to do the day of the meeting, including right before you walk in.

Of course, eventually, the time comes when you find yourself in the spotlight. Actors need to control their stage fright, hit their marks, stay present with their scene partners, and achieve what the scene has laid out for them.

Similarly, salespeople need to control their anxiety during meetings, focus deeply on their customer's pains and needs, and execute on the plan of the meeting. Instead of letting your nerves get the best of you, you'll learn how to transform that nervousness into the excitement, magic, and power of discovery. You'll also find out how to keep the focus on solving the customer's problem instead of dwelling on your own fears.

If you have struggled when it comes to handling the pricing part of a conversation, you can take comfort in knowing you are not alone. This is a common pitfall, but the good news is there are a lot of simple things you can do to handle pricing like a pro.

Eventually, of course, the meeting must end, and you need to do it with skill and purpose. Many reps do not get how to do this, so you will stand out by knowing the art of leaving your customers smiling and feeling like their time has been extremely well spent.

In enterprise selling, you will almost always need multiple meetings with a variety of titles and likely a customer trial before you can close a sale. And, of course, you will also need to stay tight with your customers on an ongoing basis to add on more sales or get a contract renewed. So I'll share best practices for all kinds of follow-up, the kind of follow-up that can make you a fortune.

Finally, the last chapter is about how to analyze your performance on an ongoing basis to constantly improve. This is what the great ones do in every profession. (And I'll share an anecdote from being on set with Steven Spielberg and Tom Cruise where this lesson was burned into my brain at an early age.) The concepts shared in this final chapter will be truly some of the most important because knowing how to get better (and truly desiring to get better) are the real keys to becoming a master of the art of sales meetings.

GO AHEAD AND DREAM BIG BECAUSE YOU CONTROL WHETHER THIS ONE COMES TRUE

If this were a book about how to become a successful actor, I could not really make any solid promises about how fast you would be successful or even that you definitely would "make it" to the upper echelon of actors with the best agents and legendary managers. There's no guarantee that you would ever get access to auditions for the most coveted roles on film, television, or stage.

In the world of acting, hard work is not the only requirement to reach the pinnacle. You also need a long apprenticeship, some big breaks, or, more likely, both. And even if you did become successful, it is no sure thing to maintain your success or even book future roles.

In the world of tech sales, it is different. I am convinced, based on practical experience, that anyone who concentrates on improving the right skills and does it with focus, passion, and hard work can become *amazingly successful*. When I say that, I mean you can earn at the elite level of top doctors, lawyers, and athletes. And it is all in your control; you just need to develop and hone your skills.

Notice that I did NOT say that it is easy to succeed in tech sales. Hard work and a hunger to succeed are absolute requirements. My point is that you have much more control over how high and far you go than you could in the acting world.

As I mentioned earlier, a healthy pipeline of quality leads will ALWAYS be necessary for sales success. But once you have mastered that, nothing will turbocharge your success faster than becoming a true master at the art of the sales meeting.

It's simple math. If your pipeline is consistently full, the way to start crushing your numbers and earn huge bonuses is to convert at a higher ratio. This is the success formula of elite tech sales warriors that crush quota every year: constantly full pipeline + convert more meetings into sales. Never let up on generating quality leads and then close them.

Nothing will separate you so much from the ordinary and average sales rep than becoming a master of meetings. And one of the best ways to do that is to understand how much the craft of acting can teach us about the art of the sales meeting.

And that's what the journey of this book will be all about. I promise you the rewards will be incredible if you are willing to hone your craft based on the principles I'll share. For those ready to take a giant leap forward, I can only say: curtains up.

CHAPTER 1

THE BLANK PAGE

*"I'm curious about other people.
That's the essence of my acting. I'm interested
in what it would be like to be you."*

—MERYL STREEP

ACTORS ARE KNOWN FOR BEING somewhat obsessed with their physical appearance (there being exceptions, of course!). I think many people make the assumption that the profession is filled with celebrities and wannabe celebrities who are narcissistic and superficial.

Vanity might be a job hazard in acting, but the truth is that most working actors diligently focus on maintaining excellent condition for a very good reason: standing up in front of people to connect and communicate with them is physically, mentally, and emotionally demanding. The typical Broadway show lights up eight times a week, the average movie can require weeks of filming with fifteen-hour days, and a network television show requires an incredibly demanding schedule stuffed into a short window of time. As the saying goes, "The show must go on," and actors quickly realize that being physically and mentally sharp is essential.

This is why you so often hear about actors hiring personal trainers, voice coaches, performance coaches, and nutrition experts. Having a healthy baseline allows an actor to bring maximum energy and focus to their work and enables them to squeeze the most out of their talent.

And this is the first and most basic comparison between the performer's craft and the art of the sales meeting. You may not be going to any audition soon, and you do not need the abs of an action hero or the timing of a comedic genius, but you do need a fundamental baseline of physical and mental health if you want to achieve meeting mastery.

Every chapter that follows in this book will dive deeper into the specifics of what you need to do to kill it in sales meetings. But before all of that, you must grasp the need for a solid foundation so you can implement everything else that follows. And that foundation starts with good overall physical and mental health, along with the right mindset.

YOUR PHYSICAL HABITS IMPACT YOUR PERFORMANCE IN MEETINGS

Consider these habits:

- Going out several nights during the work week, staying out late, and spending the following day feeling run down or hungover.
- Grabbing a fast, unhealthy lunch on a fairly regular basis because you say "you're too busy" to do anything else.
- Not blocking regular time for the gym, a run, or even for a simple, quick workout at home.

Compare that with these habits:

- Going to bed most nights at a regular time to ensure enough sleep.
- Having some "go-to" healthy quick lunches that you rely on during busy work weeks that keep you out of the fast-food drive-thru.
- Putting time for exercise as a block on your calendar.

Now do this simple thought experiment: imagine two sales reps, one with the first set of habits and the other with the second set. Think of them standing up in front of a group of C-level executives in a meeting. Which one do you think will come across as more confident? Who will come across as more focused? Which one will likely have more energy and discipline in doing their meeting preparation? Who will be able to connect with the prospective client more?

You know the answer. But knowing the right answer is worth zero points.

Your real score is based on this: which one better describes how *you* act? Are you taking good care of your overall physical health with enough sleep, regular exercise, and smart food choices? Are you doing what you need to do to perform at the best level you possibly can?

If you are struggling in this area, it's time to sit down and really ask yourself how committed you are to learning the art of the sales meeting. Since your physical health is integral to becoming your best in meetings, you need to decide which is more important to you: your bad habits or your desire to become a top tech salesperson.

You may struggle with change of this type; many do. I recommend seeking out Charles Duhigg's book, *The Power of Habit*, where he shares how folks have transformed the patterns in their mind to turn bad habits into good ones. James Clear's *Atomic Habits* is another wonderful book on this topic. It gives simple, straightforward advice that can produce profound results.

The importance of physical habits reminds me of two unique situations with sales reps I worked with who struggled in this area. The first was challenged by eating and exercise habits and would profusely sweat during meetings.

It reached the point where there would be extensive sweat marks all over his shirt by the end of meetings, and he would actually need to have a small towel to wipe himself down. Adding to the distraction was his breathing, which was as loud as any conversation going on in the room.

The other rep, I recall, was addicted to chewing tobacco. For internal company meetings, he would actually bring his spit cup into meetings. He could not do this during external customer meetings, so as a result, he would constantly bounce his legs against the table or his chair as he anxiously awaited his tobacco fix when the meeting was over.

Both of them were great people, but their habits distracted every single person in the room from reaching their potential during meetings. We were all worried about them, not the goal of the meeting and not whatever piece of technology was being sold.

You may not have an issue as extreme, but as you review this chapter, think about what physically may be holding you back from connecting deeper with your clients. What's your distraction? What may be getting in the way of communicating with clients that you can start working on today?

A couple of quick suggestions in the physical habit area. (Please remember to consult your doctor before doing any strenuous activity. Not only am I not a doctor, I don't even play one on TV!)

Yoga and stretching are valuable additions to your regular physical routines; these activities add to your overall sense of calm and strengthen your core, which is always key to controlling your physical performance. You also may want to include the opposite end of the spectrum, with things like brisk cardio, running, HITT workouts, pushups, burpees, personal trainers, group classes, etc. (In Chapter 4, we will also talk about what you can do just before a meeting to get you ready physically.)

Your Wardrobe

In the acting world, there is a concept known as "typecasting." To get typecast is to get pigeonholed to play only certain specific roles (like the gangster, the funny guy, or the pretty girl, etc.). When I was a young actor, my peers and I considered "typecast" to be a dirty word because it put a limitation on our range and talents.

We loved acting classes where we would perform demanding scenes from playwright gods like Arthur Miller, Tennessee Williams, August Wilson, Neil LaBute, Sam Shepard, Adam Rapp, and the like. Then we would leave those classes and find ourselves auditioning in the real world to play the part of the friendly neighbor with all of two lines. We did not want to be typecast in trivial roles; we wanted those meaty artistic opportunities.

But as I progressed in my acting career, I began to see there is a balance. Typecasting has a good side because it can bring steady work and allows you to develop a loyal audience. People enjoy seeing particular actors do certain kinds of roles. Think of Denzel Washington, Adam Sandler, Danny Trejo, The Rock—and even Meryl Streep. Although they all have one-off films here and there, they tend to play similar characters. In other words, they have a clear personal brand.

This applies in sales, too. Your personal brand can have a similar impact on how you are perceived by employers and prospects. For example, part of my personal brand has been to wear sharp, finely tailored suits, often blue in color.

I wear them to nearly every single kind of meeting: happy hours, internal meetings, first meetings, wrap-ups, partner visits—even sometimes on golf courses! People around me joke, "Prangley sleeps in suits."

It has served as a nice constant of my personal brand image, and it has often served as a way into conversations when people ask about it.

I am not saying everyone should adopt "almost always wearing a suit" as part of their personal brand. I know a very successful sales rep and now business owner who would often do the exact opposite. He chose clothing casual in nature, often with decals from his home state university. He made a choice for his personal brand image, and it worked well for him.

The idea you should takeaway is this: you should consciously think through your appearance choices, including clothing, shoes, and personal grooming. Whatever style you choose, invest in having a great selection of top-quality business attire for both regular meetings, as well as items appropriate for business casual events.

If you're walking into a room to ask for a million-dollar order from your clients, do you look like someone who will take care of their investment? Of course, depending on your market, your company, and your customer, this may or may not mean wearing a suit or business dress. (Unless you are me—then you are probably in a suit either way!) Standards have changed in some industries. But whatever the expectations, the requirement to show up looking very presentable should never be ignored.

Having quality clothing choices that are relevant to the customer meeting and fit you well is an aid to your confidence and will be well worth the time and money you spend on it.

In some cases, especially when selling to apparel or clothing companies, you may need to do research on what is appropriate. In my early sales days, I showed up at the headquarters of a major sporting goods company in my typical tailored suit while my prospective clients were all wearing casual brand attire. They gave me hell for it, but I also caught a break because I wasn't as far off the mark as a previous salesperson.

Apparently, several hours earlier, another sales rep had shown up to their office wearing their biggest competitor's logo. That sales rep was asked to never return. It was the simplest of mistakes, but it had a profound impact and blew any chance at a sale.

A last few points on clothing, all of which should be obvious but in my experience is sometimes overlooked.

- Clothes should always be clean of smells and stains and ironed.
- A true professional lays out their clothes the night before. That may sound like a little too much to some of you, but I have heard too many times, "I forgot I didn't have…" and miss being on time to a meeting by twenty minutes.
- You may sometimes be in the somewhat awkward position of having to discreetly share these tips with

someone who regularly goes to sales meetings with you, like your sales engineer. Be kind about it, obviously.

- If you're looking for guidance on style, I recommend reaching out to the best-dressed person in your organization who is also successful in sales. Wear a similar style, but one that still matches you (don't overdo the imitation). Also, don't feel you have to break the bank to look sharp.

- Ask for honest feedback about your clothes and presentation from the people you know care about your success. The goal is to look professional and feel confident in the clothes you wear, which still leaves a vast range of options open to all of us.

MENTAL HEALTH

Mental health is just as important as physical health—actually probably more so. Not being an expert in mental health, I am obviously not going to give you specific advice here. But I do hope that you won't hesitate to get professional assistance if you have anything that is weighing you down or holding you back.

I think most people are past the days of thinking that there should be some kind of stigma for seeking help. The sooner you address something, the quicker you can move forward productively. We should all want to solve our problems and keep working toward maximum mental and emotional health.

But don't think of mental health as only about solving problems that may require some professional assistance. There are little daily things that all of us can and should be doing to maintain mental health. Here are four suggestions for staying balanced and emotionally healthy:

1. **Daily Journaling.** I highly recommend *The Artist's Way* by Julia Cameron. It is a great read on the benefits of embracing daily writing to become aware of what's running through your head and how to take back control.

2. **Regular Breath Work.** You should be in control of the most basic function that we rely on to live. My recommendation here is *Just Breathe* by Daniel Brule.

3. **Embracing Your Hero Persona.** Set aside quiet time to imagine becoming bigger than you can imagine by breaking through personal barriers. A great resource for this is the book, *The Alter Ego Effect,* by Todd Herman. It provides great insight into how top performers leverage a simple tactic to transform into the hero they need to be.

4. **Daily Affirmations and Reviewing Your Thoughts.** Learning to own your thoughts and transforming them into powerful tools for good is an incredibly valuable habit. Ryan Holiday's book *The Daily Stoic* and Norman Vincent Peale's *The Power of Positive Thinking* are both excellent for this.

Besides physical and mental health, there's one more fundamental thing we need to talk about before you launch on your journey toward meeting mastery. It is about learning to fail, fail, fail—and then fail again. And letting that be okay, as long as you learn from it and realize it is part of the process.

GET READY TO FAIL

Understand this: becoming a master of meetings is an advanced skill. You can get competent at it in a reasonable amount of time, but to truly become great is a longer process.

That should not depress you, it should inspire you. Because it means that most people will not take the time and effort necessary to become masters in the art of sales meetings. It is tough because you will find weaknesses in yourself that you then have to address, and most won't be interested in that.

But your ability to separate yourself in this area will be a huge leap forward in your career. This is where the money, excitement, and accolades are. Wouldn't it be a terrific feeling to be in a room with multiple C-suite level executives trying to close a six-, seven-, or even eight-figure deal and feeling confident that you will do it?

However, any advanced skill that separates you from the pack is going to require a higher-level mindset. Specifically, you need to learn how to fail and fail again, without shying away from the overall challenge or flat-out quitting.

I think what happens with inexperienced sales reps is they have something embarrassing happen at a meeting (or in their head, they assume it was worse than it was), and they tell themselves, "I'm just not the type of personality that is good at running a meeting." Or they excuse themselves with the thought, "I don't need to practice this, no one else is." Or sometimes it is just about going into survival mode: "I'll just get through this and move on."

These types of excuses eventually ingrain the thought in the reps that they themselves *are* failures, instead of simply realizing that failure is a normal stepping stone to success.

This mindset is false and is so unnecessarily damaging. These reps are telling themselves a wrongheaded story based on unrealistic expectations about how fast you can achieve meeting mastery.

Of course, I would not have written this book if I did not think I could give you a roadmap to shortening your journey. If you know WHAT to work on, it is a whole lot faster to get where you want to go.

But the roadmap provided between these covers does not mean anyone can take the actual journey for you. The methods, tactics, and strategies I outline here will not mean you won't still have some painful learning, and yes, sometimes embarrassment, when you make a mistake or blunder.

Here's the thing, though. If you accept that failure is a built-in part of the path to sales meeting mastery, then you WILL eventually reach your goal. It may sound a little cliché, but in this case, it's completely true: you can only stop yourself by quitting.

Instead of telling yourself, "I'm a failure at this" or "I just don't have the right personality," tell yourself a better, truer story: "If I work hard at mastering the specific meeting skills AND I accept that failure will be a part of the process, then I will learn to crush meetings and skyrocket my close rates."

* * *

The chapter you just finished reading is one of the shortest in the book, but it is crucial that you understand that does not mean it is the least important. In fact, if you don't lay the foundation of a commitment to reasonably good physical and mental health habits, you'll never get as much out of what you'll learn in the rest of the book as you could.

Even more, if you don't have the right mindset, one that can carry you through the inevitable setbacks on the journey toward mastery, you won't get there at all. Now that you know the foundations, it's time to start digging into the practical details of getting ready for meetings.

Action Steps for Chapter 1

- Good physical health is a key part of being able to bring the appropriate energy and confidence it takes to command a room. Work on establishing and maintaining habits that promote health.

- Your wardrobe should contain quality choices for every kind of meeting. Dress in a way that is appropriate for the business culture of your prospects. And, of course, make sure your clothing is ironed, free from stains, and fresh.

- Define your personal brand with your consistent presentation.

- Do not ignore mental health issues if you are struggling. It is very difficult to achieve and sustain career success if you have an issue holding you back. For your own sake and for the good of your career, get help when needed.

- Your mindset is crucial. Remember that lots of failure is a normal and expected part of the journey toward mastering anything worth mastering!

CHAPTER 2

KNOWING
YOUR "PART"

"Luck is where opportunity meets preparation."

—DENZEL WASHINGTON

WOW, DID I FEEL FOOLISH.

I was in a meeting with another sales rep as a "wingman" and our pitch was in progress when the CEO of the company stopped us and asked a point-blank question.

"Do you know what it is we do here?"

My fellow sales rep and I exchanged glances, and we instantly knew neither of us had a good answer. What an exposed feeling! (By the way, never excuse yourself in your own mind for a lack of preparedness just because you are not the lead in the meeting. Never think, "the other person should be the one to know this." If you are in the meeting, you are responsible for at least knowing the basics.)

We managed to splutter out something about them being a media company, which was true but so vague as to be worthless. Media companies have all kinds of different models and niches, and this company made its money in a very specific way. It was crystal clear to everyone in the room that we had not done the most basic research of all.

The CEO could have—and maybe should have!—kicked us out on the spot. As salespeople, our job was to help them solve problems, and yet we didn't even know what they did. In this case, the CEO was amazing and took the time to patiently explain to us what they did and made up for our deficit of research.

As it happened, it was a very intricate business model. They were a parent organization with a lot of moving parts and sub-organizations. This revealed to us their business problem, and then we could immediately see where our solution could help.

Even if we could not have figured out that intricate model prior to the meeting through research alone, we would have at least known the right questions to ask to find out. And we wouldn't have been exposed for a lack of preparation by that simplest of questions: "Do you know what we do here?"

In the end, we landed on our feet, but that was pure luck, something you never want to rely on. We were saved by the graciousness of that CEO. Even so, I have never forgotten that experience and have made sure to never let it happen again.

Of course, knowing what a company does and how they make their money is only the most basic of basics. You are going to have to discover more.

In my acting days, I was always blown away by the degree of research leading actors would undertake to ensure they knew their characters inside out. The great Daniel Day-Lewis has a reputation for investing himself completely into his roles, including amazing amounts of research to deeply know his characters. When he played Abraham Lincoln in a Steven Spielberg film, Day-Lewis spent a year studying Lincoln's writing and speeches, went to his former home, lost significant weight to mirror Lincoln's resemblance, and modulated his voice to find Lincoln's voice. It is not a mystery why Day-Lewis creates unrivaled performances again and again. His commitment to research and his craft make the difference.

In an interview on *The Andrew Marr Show*, Day-Lewis shared this bit of wisdom about research:

> And there are many, many clues…that could bear exploration for the rest of one's days and you'd still feel there was more to learn… So I think what tends to happen is you learn as much as you can, you absorb what you learn, hope that out of that will grow something that is true. And you forget everything that you don't know…which is a lot.[1]

This quote reveals Day-Lewis's commitment to research, but also that he realizes you could do it endlessly and still never know everything. At a certain point, you have enough, and it will be time

---

[1] "Transcript: Daniel Day-Lewis on The Andrew Marr Show," *BCC News*, January 27, 2013, https://www.bbc.com/news/entertainment-arts-21139066.

to move forward. If you want to reach the point of having enough research in an efficient way, you have to know the nuts and bolts of gathering it.

THE HOW AND WHY OF RESEARCH

Research is a key part of almost every phase of the sales process, particularly in the early stages. It is definitely a key part of prospecting.

(Again, if you struggle with prospecting, I cover that topic extensively in my book, *The Tech Sales Warrior*. You have to own prospecting to be a consistently effective seller—if you blame your inside rep, the economy, the product, the customer not having time, the prospect always choosing another priority, or any number of other excuses, you will never be a consistent quota crusher that makes elite commissions. To state the obvious, if you aren't persistently excellent at filling your pipeline weekly, your meeting skills won't matter because you won't have enough of them.)

As the process moves forward into the next phase of the sales funnel, and you begin to have meetings, you will build on the research established during the prospecting phase. I cannot give you any neat division between prospecting research versus meeting research, and it really does not matter where one bleeds into the other.

The important thing is that the research gets done and that you get it down in good notes. Research should be the foundation for generating the right questions as you seek to pinpoint the specific problem you can solve for your customer.

Research on the company is crucial, but don't forget the personal aspect. Beyond the revenue growth or loss trends or other insights on the firm, how will the people you are working with be impacted? If the deal goes well and solves a big problem, will your champion inside the company get a promotion? Would your C-Suite executive prospect hit their annual bonus as a result of the project? Would it fulfill a mission or objective that will increase their standing in the firm?

There will also be some situations where a reseller partner has set you up with a potential customer, and so you did not do research during prospecting. If you find yourself in that kind of situation, good research is even more imperative. Of course leverage the insights of your partner, but do your own work as well.

This is a great scenario to be in because a reseller will generally have a wealth of knowledge to give you before you step foot into the prospect's office. On the flip side, if you embarrass a reseller with a lack of preparation and not following their guidance, how likely do you think it is that they will want to work with you again?

THE BASICS OF RESEARCH (THE HOW)

Every research situation can be a little different, but there are some basic sources and methods that apply again and again. Here is a quick guide to get you going in the right direction.

Start with the Company's Website

Start with the company's own website. Of course, these websites can be kind of sprawling, and there will be a lot of pages that will be irrelevant to your research.

Often a good place to start is the About Us section, or a company history page (often they are both on the same page). No need to go too deep here, just take in the broadest strokes. Look for things like how long the company has been around, its status as a public or private company, a general sense of how they identify it, its overall products and services, and the business model they use to make money.

You may end up referencing this kind of general research if it comes up naturally at a meeting, and that will send the message you are the kind of person who does their homework. But a lot of times, this will simply serve as good context for digging a little deeper.

You will want to continue your hunt around the website for things like mission statements, company goals, code of ethics, board statements, or anything that is a public pronouncement about their core values and their goals.

Why are these kinds of things particularly important? For one, knowing how they see themselves and their goals can give you a feel for the style and culture of a company, which can be helpful context.

But more specifically, you can use what you find to tie one of their goals to your solution. If you can help them meet a goal or solve a problem that is blocking their path toward meeting a promise to their customers, shareholders, the company's board, or to a regulatory agency, that is the research gold you are seeking.

Here is an example of what I mean:

Let's say you see a statement from the CEO on their public code of ethics that says something along the lines of "We never lose sight of putting our customers first. This applies to all levels of our company. It's the responsibility of every single employee of this company to always put our customers' interests first."

For the purposes of this example, let's say the solution you sell protects customer data from exposure and malicious use. And you know from prior conversations and research that this company has a problem with massive exposure of data.

This is a place where you can point out how your solution can bring the company in alignment with the publicly stated code of ethics and reduce liability. In short, if they say they are putting customer interest above all else, that certainly means protecting customer data.

It's very important when you go down this road of connecting a mission statement or goal back to your solution that you have a true and specific understanding of how your product can uniquely help to achieve it.

A broad statement of "we can help" or (to continue our example), "we could have saved your company from that breach," will hurt, not help, your cause. But if you use logic and provide compelling reasons on how you can truly help, you will leapfrog your competition 99 times out of 100.

One other thing to note here. Stating how you can help also means not overpromising what your product can do either. That will only come back to hurt you.

The more research you do along these lines, the more you can prove to your prospective customer that you care about helping them with their priorities. More importantly, you remind them that solving this is urgent and in line with direct statements from the highest level of leadership.

Remember to Deploy Research
with Great Care

This would be the appropriate time to give a caution about how you use what you find in your research. I want you to visualize any and all research you do as coming with a big, red warning sticker like a package carrying fragile material: Handle with Care. If you fall into the temptation of believing you absolutely KNOW something about a company, you might come across as a presumptuous know-it-all. Just as bad, you may not listen and miss crucial information about your customer's pain (much more on this later).

Don't make the assumption that everything you read on the website or find online has equal weight and is up-to-the-minute accurate. Things may have changed. Or what you assume is a major goal or mission of the company may be a lesser priority than what appears from your research.

And even if you are 100 percent accurate in what you are saying, you want to be sure not to call people out in a way that strikes a nerve that will make your customer want to close ranks and treat you like an outsider.

A better approach for deploying research would run along these lines: "You bring up a great point, it sounds like something I read on your website about your board's priorities [whatever the issue]. Would you say that this is a high priority?" Instead of beginning with a bold statement of what you know, you have turned it into a question.

If their answer reveals that it is a priority, dig in more. "How would you rank this project in importance this year, and who else on your team cares about it?"

If the answers keep coming, then don't stop. Work on getting more specific on a timeline. "And when do you need to have this completed by?" From here, you can work back from a purchase date to their project deadlines.

As you build off your research, you want to find out what happens to the company or to the individual's jobs or bonuses if nothing is done about the problem you are exploring. Basically, who would care and why? Finding out the answers to these questions will help you discover the core motivations that are so valuable as you help your customers solve important problems.

To summarize, the method you want to use is to come in with some solid research prior to the meeting and then use informed questioning combined with active listening to deepen your understanding of the problem they need solved.

When the prospect realizes that you have done your homework and are listening to their needs, it opens up a dialogue.

The customers themselves will guide you to their pain if you do this right. By having them do this introspection, it also forces your prospect to face their pain and use their own words to talk about the problem and then a potential solution. This is far superior than coming in with little to no research and then just pitching a generic product to them.

Searching for Specific Company News and General Industry Trends

Dive into news stories that mention the company you are researching. One area you definitely want to explore is financial indicators. If they are a publicly traded company, this will be easier to track down, based on stock prices and mandatory quarterly and annual reporting. However, private companies also usually have clues you can dig out from news stories and industry trends.

Whether the company is public or private, you also want to read about any positive or negative news impacting the company's reputation in the marketplace. If your product or service can help to directly solve a negative issue or contribute toward a solution, this is valuable research. This is another place to deploy research with great care, however.

You never want to come across as exploiting negative publicity. You may know something extremely damning about your prospect, but let them share it with you. Use your research to build great questions in advance to tease the answers that will open the conversation. Also, keep in mind that many companies will need a signed

Non-Disclosure Agreement (NDA) in place before opening up fully to your discovery questions. In these cases, you may need to lead more of your questions with hypotheticals and generalities just to get your customer talking. A great way to do this is to leverage a real-world case study that parallels their pain.

Another option is to show a technical solution in your demo for the exact issue they are facing. The point is to get your prospect talking more about their pain.

Another avenue to explore are trends in their industry in general. Are there certain circumstances that are impacting every company in the industry? Baselines or risk scores that they would care about? This could be everything from a baseline of risk to protecting specific data types to accelerating a process. How are other companies in their industry addressing the problem your solution solves? If a meeting is too quiet, bring it alive by exploring these questions.

This kind of research can go in different directions depending on the industry and the company, but at a minimum, you want to understand the current challenges in their marketplace so you can ask intelligent questions in meetings.

Human Sources

Getting information from people with direct knowledge of the company is usually the best kind of research. This is not always an option, but when it is, make sure you gather it.

For example, if you work with a reseller or ecosystem technology partners, they probably know some of the key personalities at the company you'll be meeting with. Find out from them who is likely to be at the meeting, and ask questions about individual communication styles, likes and dislikes, and outside interests.

You may also already have an ally within the company who is your champion for your deal. They can give you some insight into the people involved and a more granular view of the problems they need your solution to solve.

They may also have priceless insights into personal challenges or goals of the people who will be involved in the meeting—the same folks who could champion your solution. For example, let's say a CISO who has a goal to do "X" by year-end and will receive a bonus in the amount of $XXX if the project is complete. Knowing that could be valuable in figuring out the timing of the deal and getting it across the finish line. When you can align to personal ambition, goals, and needs, your project can move up the priority list.

Special Tools

Many companies pay for special research tools that can go deeper with insights than you can find in a Google search. These tools are too often ignored. Companies are paying anywhere from a few thousand dollars to millions a year for access to this information, so it is silly not to take advantage of it.

These tools are sophisticated and can predict things like buying intent (a.k.a. "intent data"), which can be a way to get a read on how urgent your product or service may be for a prospective customer.

As much as I encourage you to use these tools for your research, there is one caveat. Things can change rapidly at any company in terms of priority and objectives, so any information can become dated quickly, even from the best of tools.

As with every area, always ask good discovery questions in meetings to confirm your research. Triangulate what you learn from different sources (resellers, technology partners, and your champion within the prospective company) to make sure you are on the right path.

One further note. It's also important not to get lost in hours of research during prime business hours that may impact the time you need for prospecting, meetings, and closing existing deals. Research through technology is one of those things meant to be done outside of prime time so you maximize your time during the day.

Social Media Accounts

Social media can be helpful for research in two ways. One, check the social media accounts of the company itself. Be careful not to go down too many rabbit holes because much of what is posted there will be completely irrelevant. But you will find some great nuggets, and it can give you a clue to the culture of the company. You may also find positive company news linked from their social media accounts, including insights on philanthropic events they support. It may be a good time to start volunteering.

The other value of social media is as a source of profiles of meeting participants. LinkedIn is, of course, the best for this. Entering the company name in the search field can yield a plethora of profiles that will have key information on meeting participants.

Look up those who will be in the meeting. Have they recently liked or shared a post? Or posted original content? Look for common connections, their educational background, their interests, and other data about what the person cares about. Take down notes for yourself so you can review it prior to heading into your meeting.

If your firm pays for LinkedIn's premium offering, Sales Navigator, be sure to use it because it has a ton of value. There is so much more you can add to your arsenal with this tool: targeted advertising, heat maps, tracking job moves, direct messaging capabilities to decision makers, detailed reporting and exporting, and more.

Some of what you find will be valuable, and some of it won't. But doing your homework pays off if even just one bit of it advances your knowledge of the company. The more you know, the better chance you will be able to help find their pain and help them solve problems.

I remember working with a sales rep on an upcoming meeting with a groundbreaking automotive manufacturer. For these innovative manufacturers, intellectual property is everything.

Tensions were heightened around this issue when news headlines revealed that a top engineer in this industry stole intellectual property secrets from one firm. Knowing this allowed us to get specific when we went into the meeting.

The meeting immediately lit up when we said, "We recently worked at another leading firm in your space that struggled to identify who could access their data and who was changing access to their data. When the board asked for a quick report, the IT team wasn't able to provide it. They had all the best-of-breed logging software solutions, including 'X, Y, Z,' yet they still could not answer this simple question in a timely fashion and as a result the security of their IP was unknown. Does this sound familiar?"

Answer: "Yes, in fact, we are facing a similar problem now. Can you share how your platform integrates with Azure Active Directory and if it can do X, Y, and Z? We have an immediate need to be responsive to our board, too." The entire room opened up from there, and the questions multiplied.

That's a good overall outline of how to do research and then how to deploy it in a meeting.

Overall, my advice is to not think of research as an exact science but more like being a detective on a mission. Keep your antenna up as you search around, looking for those places that reveal useful insight into the players and pain at the company you are scouting. Like most skills, the more you do it, the better feel you will get for what you need, how much you need, and where you need to explore.

Trust your gut. If you feel like you're clueless walking into a meeting, you probably are. If you feel like you have a good sense of the company, you probably do, although sometimes do a touch more just to be safe. But if you're ready to write a book report on the firm, you probably have done too much.

A good rule of thumb: If you can talk about how the firm makes money, its goals for the year, and recent challenges, you're off to a great start. In other words, don't overthink this too much. Instead, think of Goldilocks and the search for "just right."

THE GOLDILOCKS PRINCIPLE OF RESEARCH

As much as I emphasize the importance and value of researching your customers, you want to aim to do the right amount. Do enough to have quality information but not so much that you become inefficient.

If you underdo it, you will not be prepared and you will blow opportunities. On the other hand, if you spend too much time on research, you are wasting your precious time.

You won't always get this perfect, but the more you do it, the more you will get a feel for the "just right" amount of research.

If you build it up in your mind as something that is difficult and time-consuming, you will procrastinate and avoid it. Once you make research a regular habit, you will become more and more efficient at it. Use the tips above, and you will be well on your way.

THE BIG, OFTEN OVERLOOKED BENEFIT OF SOLID RESEARCH

It is worth briefly examining WHY you do research. Of course, in one sense, I hope the "why" is 100 percent obvious to any tech salesperson. You want to know enough about the company to be able to talk intelligently to your customers and to demonstrate you care enough about earning their business.

But there is a benefit on top of those more obvious benefits, one that is less tangible but still very real. The more you know about a company and the personalities involved, the more confident you will be. When you "wing it," it is not just your customers who will know it. You know it internally, too, and it will make you nervous. When you come in having done the proper amount of homework, it gives you a confident edge. As humans, we naturally pick up on confidence when we see it, and we also sense the lack of it.

There's one more aspect to research and your customers. It is something I learned from my training as an actor, and I think it has lessons for sales, too.

NO JUDGMENT ZONE

As I noted above, actors do research, too. You research the character you will be playing through various means. This first step is to dive into the script and the world of the characters to understand their history and their choices. You learn about your characters from what they say and from how they interact with the other characters. But that's just the beginning.

There are different philosophies of how to research your character and their emotional experience so you can transform yourself into the character. For example, there is what many refer to as "method acting," where you use your own personal history to access the emotions that your character is experiencing.

There are other ways and schools of acting to get to know your character, like through historical research, your own imagination, a deep study of folks living a life like your character, or perhaps even by replicating how they lived their life for a period of time. In the end, research into a character is about finding why your character says and does the things they do. You want to *understand* them.

And this brings us to one of the secrets of great acting, and it is a skill directly relevant to sales. The secret is this: never judge the character you are playing. The goal is to always understand them, never to judge them.

If your character is a villain—even the epitome of evil—your job is not to sit in judgment. The reason for this is simple. Everyone is the hero from their own perspective. So if you think, "I judge this character to be evil: I have to figure out how to be evil," then you won't be playing that character from how it really feels inside them.

When I transitioned to sales, I realized that judgment is also a bad idea when it comes to sales meetings. Just like with acting, you want to understand your customers, not judge them. The only difference is this: instead of researching a character so you can bring them to life, you are researching your customers so you can understand their perspective on the problem you are trying to solve.

That abrasive potential customer who is gruffly questioning you? Maybe his job is on the line if he doesn't solve a technical security issue, and he wants to be 100 percent sure your product will solve it. Perhaps he was burnt recently by a sales rep that over-promised and under-delivered their solution. Or maybe he has found that having an edge with people has been an effective technique for getting what he wants. Maybe he's just having a bad day.

If you were coming from an angle of judgment, you could decide that those reasons justify gruff behavior or that they don't. But you aren't going to waste energy doing that. Instead, you are going to keep your focus on discovering what problem you can solve for the person in front of you.

The second you start judging, you are setting yourself up to react emotionally. And the more emotional you are, the less chance you will stay focused on what you need to accomplish in a meeting. That's bad enough.

But you also lose the opportunity to understand the perspective of the other person. The more you can understand their perspective, the more you have insights on how to connect with them. This builds rapport that separates you from the pack of reps attempting to earn their business through canned sales demos.

I remember a particularly good exercise for this when I was being trained as an actor. We were required to read a book called *Spoon River Anthology* by Edgar Lee Masters. It was a portrait of over two hundred characters in two small towns, using poems to dive deep into the experiences and points of view of each character. As we read, we found that we judged less and understood more because we could see how life looked through the eyes of very different individual characters, each with their own sets of challenges and triumphs.

Do you have to read *Spoon River Anthology* to master meetings? Of course not. (Although it might not hurt, either!) The crucial lesson is to work on getting inside another's perspective and to commit to an understanding mindset, not one of judgment. None of us are perfect in this area, as judging seems to come more naturally to humans than understanding.

However, when you make a point to practice putting yourself in the mind and feelings of others, you will be better prepared to stay focused on problem-solving.

Make this one of your mantras: "I'm not going to judge; I'm going to understand. And I will stay focused on how I can help the person(s) in front of me."

RESEARCH + UNDERSTANDING = CONFIDENCE

To sum up this chapter in the most concise way possible: you cannot expect to be confident and in command at meetings if you do not have a foundation of research to draw upon to ask good questions.

Just as importantly, you cannot get caught up in assumptions and judgments about your customers. The point of research and discovery is always to understand. This keeps emotional reaction on your part to a minimum and allows you to stay laser-focused on solving problems for customers.

With research as a foundation, it is time to head into the equivalent of the actor's studio and figure out how you are going to craft your pitch.

Action Steps for Chapter 2

- Good research allows you to ask the right questions of your prospective customers to uncover pain and find solutions. Without it, you will be stuck with a very generic presentation that will not connect with your prospects.

- Research is especially valuable when you find a way to connect a company mission or a personal goal (hitting a bonus, etc.) to the problem you solve.

- As important as research is, it should not be done during prime business hours. Those hours are better spent on prospecting and meetings.

- The more you sharpen your research skills, the better you will get at spending the right amount of time on it. There comes a point when you have done enough and any more becomes inefficient. If your company pays for quality tools that aid your research, use them.

- Remember that you are not there to judge your prospective customers; you are there to understand them. Focus on discovery and problem-solving.

CHAPTER 3

THE LAB

Crafting and Practicing Your Pitch

"The actor has to develop his body.
The actor has to work on his voice.
But the most important thing the actor
has to work on is his mind."

—STELLA ADLER

WHEN I GOT SERIOUS ABOUT my training as an actor, I had to decide between chasing an MFA through a university or building my own plan by enrolling in an acting studio. People often assume that actors simply go to college for training, but the truth is much of the best acting training (and ongoing coaching) happens in actor studios in New York and Los Angeles. Even schools like New York University (NYU) send their enrolled students to various studios throughout the city to deepen their understanding of methods for performing.

I decided to go the actor studio route directly and was fortunate enough to get accepted into the William Esper Studio two-year conservatory program in Manhattan, and there I studied with the remarkable Terry Knickerbocker (as well as some other truly fantastic teachers).

Terry built a reputation for over twenty-five years at Esper and as a faculty member for NYU's experimental theater wing. Today he runs his own studio (TKS) in Brooklyn, New York, and has coached Sam Rockwell, Michelle Williams, John Leguizamo, Boyd Holbrook, Chris Messina, and other great talents.

Terry was the kind of teacher who would not let you slide if you were not well prepared for that day's work. Class was tough, eye-opening, and rewarding. At first, I didn't understand why we would have to sit through and watch others perform instead of just showing up for our own performances, but in time I realized how watching others perform and receive coaching helps you get better, too.

One of the biggest lessons I learned—and it is directly relevant for sales meetings—is that there are so many nuances in communication that we either fail to notice or just take for granted. The acting craft explores all of these nuances in great depth to the point where a simple conversation feels almost like a martial art.

Being challenged to get better in a difficult art will sometimes create emotional fallout. In several of our scene study classes together, fellow actors would break down or storm out of the room in anger or disappointment as they faced their own resistance, a deficiency in their current skill set, or just plain old public embarrassment at their own lack of preparation.

But his students accepted that turmoil because Terry had that special quality that all great teachers have. You knew he cared about you as a person and about helping you get better at your craft. (If you are lucky enough to find a sales mentor who fits this description, be appreciative and cultivate that relationship!)

There are two things that were particularly crucial that I learned studying with Terry, and both those lessons carried over when I transitioned to sales.

The first lesson is the importance of having a space to learn and fail. The studio was a playground, but one we took super seriously. It was scheduled, it required hours of preparation, and demanded complete attention when you were there. Terry made the studio a place to bring your best self, to push yourself to the limits of your current ability, and then inevitably fail much of the time. That's what happens when you dare to go outside your comfort zone—you fail and learn. If you do it enough times, you will eventually grow into an artist and craftsman at what you do.

The problem for actors, though, is that when you fail, it can be extremely public and dramatic. Terry was willing to let you go as far as your current skill could take you and then choose that moment to firmly push you to go further.

And we let him push us because we knew that it was never about humiliating us, it was about making us better at our craft.

Throughout this book, I will give you skills you must develop. You need to create a place where you can work on those skills without fearing humiliation. Sometimes that may just be your own mirror or watching a video recording of your work at home. Maybe it will involve a trusted colleague, friend, or mentor. If your team does role-playing and skill-building using meeting scenarios, take it seriously and get the most out of it.

Of course, just like an actor has to eventually take to the stage or screen, you will also have the courage to push yourself to be better in live meetings. It cannot always be a playground, but having a place for skill practice is invaluable.

The second lesson from my time studying with Terry is that you are more powerful than you imagine. And the key to unlocking that power is hard work, research, and more hard work. As you master the skills, you reach a level where you can be fully present in the moment of performance, and that is one of the most exciting feelings you will ever have.

How did this carry over into my sales career? While you are not performing for your customers, the skills you use to communicate and interact in a meeting are extremely similar to the tools you use as an actor. You can learn to be fully present to your customers and colleagues when running a meeting, and mastering particular skills is how you get there. When you are able to train yourself to be fully present, any feelings of drudgery toward your job go away, and you are left feeling amped and excited about what you do.

That is what is at the end of this road for you if you commit yourself to the art of the sales meeting. I hope that inspires you.

If you are inspired, the next question is, what specifically do you work on? Assuming you have done the research, the next step is crafting your pitch.

THE TWO SIDES OF PREPARING AND EXECUTING A PITCH

A pitch has two main components. One component is the actual words you say. The other component is all the actions, gestures, tone, etc., that you use to communicate non-verbally. In my experience, reps make a couple of key mistakes here. When they think about the actual words they say, they think of it as a script detached from themselves. They are not putting enough effort to understand the meaning behind what they are saying and how it will connect with the prospect in front of them.

The other mistake is just as bad, if not worse. They completely ignore the non-verbal communication aspect. That is a huge mistake, and it is why meetings are so often draining and boring for all involved. A little later in the chapter, I will share all the non-verbal skills you will want to develop.

First, though, let's talk about the words you will prepare for your pitch. We all understand that the words we use are important, but unfortunately, that doesn't often translate into creating a good pitch.

That's because many sales reps think of pitch preparation as similar to memorizing a script word-for-word to "get it perfect." Unfortunately, this practice results in pitches that fall flat. Words have maximum power when we back them up with meaningful thought. That is the secret of great orators like John F. Kennedy and Martin Luther King, Jr.

Let me give you a quick, simple exercise that you can literally do right now. First, say these words out loud: "I am awesome." Note internally to yourself how that feels.

Now do this. I want you to think about all the awesome things you have done over the past year. It could be something you have done to get stronger inside for yourself, or it can be things you did for others, or both. Say at least three of them out loud right now.

Next, write those things down. Reread them to yourself. Say those accomplishments out loud one more time. When you hear them, do they inspire you? (If not, go back to the drawing board and come up with some other awesome things you have done.) You may even have to ask a loved one to share three awesome things they love about you.

After you have come up with your three compelling things, written them down, said them out loud twice, and reread them, I want you to think of them as you again say out loud, "I am awesome."

Compare how you feel to the first time you said it just a few minutes ago. For some people, it is a slight change of feeling, and for others, it is more dramatic, but most people notice the impact.

Why is there a difference? Because you took a little more time to connect the words coming out of your mouth to deeper underlying truth and meaning.

Now try this with your pitch. Pick out a key sentence or two and say them out loud. Next, ask things like:

- "What do these words mean to me?"
- "How do I relate to them—have I seen them in action with customers or heard the power of them through case studies?"
- "Have you heard or seen customers' lives transform when they do these things? What did that look like? What did their faces look like as they realized your product could solve a huge problem for them?"

After reflecting on your answers to these questions, return to the one or two sentences from the pitch and say them out loud. You will feel more connected to the words, and more empowered to say them. Does it feel like you are sharing special news? It's exciting because you have grounded it in a powerful experience. If that's not happening, keep working on that part of the pitch until you do feel it.

Go through the pitch section by section doing this until you feel confident and connected to every important point. (And being that you don't want to waste anyone's time, every part should be important—cut anything that is not.)

It's helpful when practicing the pitch in this way to use a video camera or trusted partner with great communication skills to show you the truth about your performance.

When your pitch is authentic, your prospect will feel it. This was another interesting revelation in acting classes: when authentic emotions are shared in scenes, the audience feels the same type of emotions the actors are feeling. Part of being human is that we absorb the true feelings of those around us. That's definitely true in your sales meetings.

You need to ask yourself: what type of presence have you been bringing to your meetings? How much meaning are you bringing to the words you are saying? Are you connecting with others in the room on a regular basis? If you aren't, you need to keep working on the mastery of your pitch.

Remember to trust your gut as you work through the pitch. If it feels like filler, it is. If you feel bored, tired, or confused with your material, I guarantee your audience will feel the same.

A sales engineer at a previous company I worked with many years ago had such a boring tone that folks would literally fall asleep when he would speak or while he would walk through demos in his meetings. At best, his prospects would shut off their cameras and do other work. It was boring. Impersonal. Out of touch. And even with many notes of hope and help, he never took ownership of this meeting deficiency. Would you want to buy what he's selling? I'm not sure *he* was sure he wanted to buy what he was selling.

Doing all the upfront work to make sure you are not boring can feel scary when you are not used to it. But when embraced with consistent practice, it becomes a lot of fun, and as a result, you will feel more confident, empowered, and present in your meetings.

This recalls an example from when I was a front-line manager at a previous company. I went to a meeting with a young rep to shadow his development.

As the meeting kicked off, the sales rep opened his laptop, and I could see his body tensing, his hands clamming up. I could tell we were headed for trouble.

For the next fifteen minutes, he proceeded to pitch the customer by reading the corporate notes section on each slide verbatim. One agonizing slide by one agonizing slide. He never asked a single question and never looked up. In fact, he was so nervous he kind of turtled his head behind the screen.

I jumped in shortly after this intro to save what we could from the meeting. Afterward, I connected with the rep for direct feedback. When I asked what happened, he said, "I just wanted to get it right."

I asked him if he could see what his audience was doing while he read. He said no. When I told him they weren't listening, he was taken aback. "Really? Not at all?"

When the prospects realized the rep was just reading, they tuned out, and their cell phones became better entertainment. This is a somewhat extreme example, but I can tell you it is a common mistake to think that reading the approved corporate text is the pitch.

The job is not to read the right things; the job is to discover problems and solve them for your customers. And you'll never do that hiding behind a laptop or following a cookie-cutter script that means nothing to you personally.

Unfortunately, I've also witnessed similar behavior in virtual meetings. An inexperienced rep may think that it is safer to turn the camera off, but the human ear picks up the rhythm of your voice and can tell the differences between words read off a page versus having an authentic conversation.

With this kind of "read the pitch" mentality (whether live or virtual), you will usually miss when a prospective customer interrupts your pattern with an interesting question. You either don't hear it, don't understand it, or lose your place. I have seen rooms go silent as a rep says, "Sorry, I lost my spot." If you know your pitch and the meaning behind the words, that won't happen, and you'll be able to adjust on the fly.

THE RIGHT WAY TO CRAFT A PITCH

I cannot give you a one-size-fits-every-situation way to put together the right words for a pitch. The whole point is that you should be customizing your company pitch to the situation (i.e., happy hour, first meeting, follow-up, closing meeting, elevator pitch, etc.). What I can do, however, is give you some solid guideposts for how to work through the planning of a customized pitch.

1. Analyze What You Know Already and Always Be as Targeted as Possible

Plan on uncovering as much of the problem that the customer needs solved as early on in the pitch as possible. So as you prepare, write down what you know already about their problem and then what discovery questions you want to ask based on that knowledge.

In some cases, you may already know a lot about the problem. Maybe a reseller partner or the customer provided you with a lot of information and data about the problem prior to the meeting. In this case, begin building your case for how your product can solve the problem with the specifics you have in hand. Consider how you will handle detours to get back to your main message using great questions.

It is so much more impressive to come in with a customized presentation showing what you can do for this specific customer based on their needs rather than deliver some general fluff about your company.

One word of warning here, however. As you plan out your pitch, remember that even if you have a lot of information, you should not assume you understand the full extent of your customer's pain and the problems they need solved. If you assume too much, you will leave information on the table.

Plan out additional discovery questions to build on what you know, and listen for the clues from your prospect so you can address their specific needs. And reminder, you can't pick up on cues and listen properly if your eyes are glued to a screen reading!

2. Do Memorize Your Company's
General Pitch

Despite the fact that I strongly recommend against a bland, vanilla pitch, it is still important that you know the standard pitch of your company backwards and forwards. Having it locked into your head gives you a base of knowledge to draw from in many different scenarios, and then you can choose what is relevant for the people in front of you. Knowing all the parts of the company pitch is like having a bunch of tools in your toolbox, and you can confidently pull out the right one for any situation. Most importantly, it keeps your eyes up and engaged with the room.

If part of your standard pitch includes a general PowerPoint presentation, plan to use it when appropriate and practice going through it so you can deliver it smoothly. But here again, you will want to customize it for your audience.

Use the slides that are needed to achieve the goal of the meeting. For instance, a reseller partner may tell you that a particular CISO doesn't like hearing anything about the background of the company, employee count, financials, etc. Then avoid using these slides.

Either way, never spend a lot of time on background company information. When delivered poorly and at length, it screams everything people hate about sales. A best practice is to use this background information sparingly, on request, and keep it to under thirty seconds.

3. Plan Out the Case Studies That Will Resonate with Your Prospective Customer

Use all your prior research and any information you have gathered to reflect on what case studies may be most appropriate. If you have enough information going in, the perfect case study may be clear. In that case, meticulously plan out how you will present it and really nail it.

In situations where you have more limited information, have a few at your fingertips and use any that are applicable as the meeting reveals what case study or studies are the best match(es).

As a general goal, you should build up your knowledge of your company's case studies to the point where you can confidently and clearly deliver an example wrapped inside a case study story for almost any situation.

Let's take a small detour to emphasize the importance of storytelling. For thousands of years, human beings have connected over storytelling. Think of your favorite film, novel, childhood fable, speech, a time around a fire with friends swapping stories, an old tale from a grandparent—the list could go on for quite some time.

We crave them, and they connect us. In a sales setting, the right story can show an organization how your product can change its company. It might be an epic tale of transformation or a quieter tale about an opportunity seized.

The key point is that case studies and storytelling are powerful, and you need to master them. Know at least three case studies and your company's origin story extremely well so you can pitch with passion at a moment's notice. If you'd like to dive deeper into the profound power of storytelling, a few wonderful books on the topic are: *The Power of Myth* by Joseph Campbell; *The Writer's Journey* by Christopher Vogler; *Made to Stick* by Chip Heath and Dan Heath; and *Stories that Stick by Kindra Hall.*

I also strongly recommend an article from the *Harvard Business Review* entitled "Storytelling That Moves People." From the article:

> Customers must be convinced to buy your company's products or services, employees and colleagues to go along with a new strategic plan or reorganization, investors to buy (or not to sell) your stock, and partners to sign the next deal. But despite the critical importance of persuasion, most executives struggle to communicate, let alone inspire. Too often, they get lost in the accouterments of company speak: PowerPoint slides, dry memos, and hyperbolic missives from the corporate communications department. Even the most carefully researched and considered efforts are routinely greeted with cynicism, lassitude, or outright dismissal.

Later in this article, one of the most well-known screenwriting coaches, Robert McKee, shares this:

> ...executives can engage listeners on a whole new level if they toss their PowerPoint slides and learn to tell good stories instead...ultimately a much more powerful way is by uniting an idea with an emotion. The

best way to do that is by telling a compelling story. In a story, you not only weave a lot of information into the telling but you also arouse your listener's emotions and energy.[2]

To summarize your pitch preparation, the thing that matters most is to make it as relevant and customized to the specific customer as possible, and plan to relate your pitch to their problem as quickly as possible. Remember that the customer is only going to get interested when they see how what you are offering is directly relevant to their goals, to their needs.

WHAT MESSAGES ARE YOU SENDING NON-VERBALLY?

Avoiding bland, boilerplate pitches is one thing. But just as important is your delivery of those words. All the subtle, and sometimes not so subtle, signals you send non-verbally.

This is one of the most crucial concepts in the entire book and the key to seeing the connection between an actor's tools of performance and the skills that will make you a master of meetings.

To reinforce this point, I want you to do a little simple experiment for me the next time you are out in a public place, and you have a little extra time. Sit in a coffee shop, a public park, or mall

---

[2] Bronwyn Fryer, "Storytelling That Moves People," *Harvard Business Review*, June 2003, https://hbr.org/2003/06/storytelling-that-moves-people.

and look at individuals and see what signals they are sending by how they dress, their gestures, their use of voice, and their interaction with others.

What can you tell from this? How much is a person—a total stranger—revealing to you without you knowing a single word they are saying? This is not about trying to judge the people you are observing with the intent of looking down on them. (Remember from the last chapter that actors should never judge their characters, and you should not judge your customers.)

This is about understanding that humans communicate crucial information in so many ways that are independent of the words coming out of our mouths. So just watch people and let this lesson soak in.

Then take that lesson a step further and do a little additional thought experiment. Ask yourself what messages you send when you walk into a meeting. And what messages are you sending with the tone and decibel of your voice when you start speaking? How is your eye contact, and what is it saying to each person in the meeting?

Thinking about your communication in this way applies to way more than acting or sales. It impacts every area of your life.

I recently saw an interview with University of Connecticut women's basketball legendary head coach Geno Auriemma. "We put a huge premium on body language and if your body language is bad, you will never get in the game," he said. "When I watch game film, I'm checking what's going on with the bench and if someone is asleep over there, somebody doesn't care, somebody is not engaged in the game, they will never get in the game. Ever! And they know that, they know I'm not kidding."[3]

The bottom line is this:

If you can understand that communication is about much more than just the words you are saying, you will have taken a huge leap forward in your journey toward mastering the art of meetings.

Many reps I've encountered struggle to understand or study these communication concepts on a deep level. They do understand that certain public speaking skills can be helpful, but in general, they stay on the surface and miss the opportunity before them.

A great example of this was a partner rep I worked with who had a decade of selling under his belt. He worked for high-profile cyber security firms and had the ego to go with it, but strangely after nine months at his new job, he still couldn't get a deal or a trial booked to save his life.

He reached out to me for some help, and I told him I would gladly join his call in silent mode and follow up with him later if I had any feedback. What I witnessed was a rep who was friendly but overly so. He connected with his prospect on the surface level and seemed to congratulate himself for that. "Oh, you like the Bears?" "Great, so do I." "Urlacher was a beast." "What do you think about

---

[3] theLLaBB, "Body Language Matters - Geno Auriemma on Body Language and the Type of Players He Recruits," YouTube video, 2:38, https://www.youtube.com/watch?v=tp4mIONS51E.

the upcoming Bulls season?" "What's your favorite part of the city?" and on and on it went.

Twenty minutes into the meeting and having learned nothing about his customer's problem, he finally said, "I guess we should start then, huh?" You would think at this point he would dig into discovery questions or some other substance, but instead, he dove into a case study of stunning irrelevance.

It was sloppy, inaccurate, confusing, lacked clarity, and offered no value to the conversation—and it ate up another ten minutes of the meeting. The delivery came across as a child performing for his parents in the hopes they would tell him how wonderful he did. You never want to come across as someone yearning for friendship or attention; always be the person who is there to solve a problem.

No surprise that nothing came of this presentation. No trial happened, and no follow-up occurred. This was simply a case of a rep who didn't understand his material, didn't prepare his material, and rather than seeking help on his craft and working on his pitch, he decided to wing his meetings with charisma.

This idea is based on a bad stereotype of salespeople as "schmoozers." Talking sports or hobbies, getting friendly, and telling stories as if you are the funniest person in the room (or think you are) is not a substitute for substance. And substance matters. If you think that sales is some circus act, you are going to end up with a very short career.

Let's look at how we can avoid the above and go deeper into our craft.

FIFTEEN SKILLS FOR CONDUCTING
MASTERFUL MEETINGS

Becoming a true master at running meetings is not about natural talent or luck. Talent never hurts, but I would always bet on the person who works hard at developing these skills over someone who counts on natural charisma. Your ultimate success does not depend on talent (whether you think you have it or not). All that matters is your commitment to learning these specific skills.

To develop true mastery will, of course, require practice and experience, but it sure helps if you first know where to best apply your efforts. That's why I provide explanations for each of the fifteen skills below, so you'll know where to focus on improving. If you take the time to absorb and move toward mastering each of them, you will completely distinguish yourself from the overwhelming majority of sales reps.

How does conquering these skills make such a huge impact in your ability to run successful sales meetings?

Let me draw again on acting experiences to provide some helpful insight. As an actor, you cannot just memorize a script and expect to give an excellent performance based on just knowing your lines. (Although, of course, actors do need to know their lines, the same as you need to have your basic pitch down cold.)

The lines from the script are only one part of what is being communicated in a scene. Great actors communicate with so much more, using a full repertoire of tools. Without always realizing it consciously, the audience is impacted by facial expressions, body language, how actors use their voices, the way a scene is entered and exited, their actions—the list goes on.

Actors are intentional about evoking these responses. The outcomes arise through study, research, and commitment to the material. Actors are trained to embody the words and bring them to life through the character they are playing.

The meaning and communication that happen on stage and screen are heightened further from the organic interaction between actors. Excellent acting demands playing off the emotions, body language, and other non-verbal cues that come from fellow actors.

Even if you have zero acting background, I am sure none of this comes as a big surprise to you because you have witnessed terrific acting in your favorite movies and shows. You know intuitively that with great actors, there's something special about how they communicate with their audience and fellow actors that goes well beyond words. It's something that can not only be heard and seen, but felt.

Now take this one step further and apply it to your own situation as someone who presents and pitches at meetings. The magic happens when you apply these insights and skills to your own communication skills. When you improve each of these fifteen skills I am about to share, it will massively impact your ability to be in control of meetings and to get responses like, "that's the best meeting I've ever had "thank you for being efficient" and "you really listened and delivered" and "I wish all of our vendors were like this" and "Wow, we need this solution" and "I'd like to get the next meeting on the calendar right now" and "I need to pull more people from the executive team into the room—this is amazing." Even better than great comments is when you start closing more sales.

The key is realizing that running a successful meeting means much more than speaking a formulaic pitch, in the same way that top-quality acting is about much more than memorizing a script. Here are just a few examples that will help you go from merely speaking lines to totally confident presentations:

- Preparing your instrument (you) before you walk into the room
- Reading and mirroring back body movements to sync with others in the room
- Connecting to your material so that you understand and can visualize the impact of each word
- Using listening skills to guide your speed and next move throughout your presentation
- Feeling present and alive in the room because you know your material so well you can jump from topic to topic at ease

There's one more thing to be aware of before we dive into the specific list of skills. Do not expect yourself to be good or even competent at all fifteen of these immediately. Many of these are advanced skills that will take some time before you can become comfortable executing on them like a polished pro. And remember, this isn't about trickery, but rather, mastering clear and effective communication to make the most of your and your customer's time.

However, you should be able to dramatically reduce the time necessary to master them because you will know exactly what skills to focus on and sharpen. You also do not need to tackle them all at once. As you get more practice and experience, you will be able to add more and more of them.

Fifteen Skills to Master

In a way, these fifteen skills are a summary and a roadmap to this whole book. Much of the rest of this book expands on how to get better at these individual skills. If you are serious about using this book as a tool for continuous improvement, come back to this list often and ask yourself how you can keep getting better at each one. It is your blueprint for building mastery.

1. Listening

It is easy to say, "You have to be a better listener," and it can even sound like a bit of a cliché. But this is something that you can train yourself to do by making a serious effort to give 100 percent attention to whoever is speaking. You have heard of great eye contact; think of this as making great ear contact.

It is typical for all of us to tend toward thinking about what we want to say while the other person is still talking. Break yourself of this. If this worries you because you think you won't have a timely response, try this. When the other person finishes, repeat a few things back to the person, and they will know you were listening. It also buys you a break so you can formulate an intelligent response.

I remember working with an amazing rep who was a leader in prospecting and always at the top of the pack when it came to getting quality meetings. But strangely, her conversion rates to trial were among the lowest.

After shadowing a few of her meetings, it was clear she had a great grasp of the pitch and also asked great discovery questions. The trouble was she failed to use the answers she received to inform her next question or to adjust her presentation to match the client's concerns.

It was a classic case of not listening well. It was as if the customer handed her a gift, and she threw it on the floor. This is where good sales reps have the opportunity to become great ones—by listening and then marrying the words of their prospects' pain to the words of the solution they sell.

2. The Use of Inflection

Inflection is one of those things that is tough to describe in writing, but just being mindful of it will help you improve. We will talk about recording yourself at the end of this chapter, and inflection is definitely an area where recording can reveal important things to you.

There is another actor's tool that can have an impact here. Have you ever seen a great performance where an actor in the middle of an extremely heated, emotional moment will not raise their voice at all but, instead, deliver a line in an almost subtle monotone? It increases the impact despite the lowered tone.

Using an exceptionally calm voice when delivering a specific statement that is intense on its own can serve to highlight it. If you try to use an overly dramatic tone, you can actually lessen your effect. If you are talking about a serious problem the customer has that needs to be solved, or people will lose their jobs, try using a soft inflection to show more empathy.

The opposite of this is to not consider inflection at all, which is simply boring. I mentioned earlier the sales engineer who was so monotone customers and his own team would fall asleep during meetings. I know you are probably thinking I am exaggerating. People fell asleep listening to the guy talk?

Oh, it happened and happened often. Do you think this person ever hit quota, let alone ever crushed quota? No, he didn't. Inflection is critical in controlling the impact of your words and, ultimately, the outcome of your meetings.

3. Efficiency of Words

This has several aspects:

One, always practice being crisp and clear in how you speak. It can help to have the standard parts of the pitch down cold and practice the custom parts as needed.

Two, answer the question that was asked without going on and on about things that were not in the question. Too many reps are nervous and begin babbling extraneous information.

Three, challenge yourself to get better and better about using fewer words. Try to be the Hemingway of tech salespeople. You will be surprised how fast you can make progress in this area when you simply focus on being more efficient in how you express yourself. You might at first be horrified by how much you ramble once you begin to focus on being more efficient, but use that horror to get better.

The *New York Times* bestselling author Robert Greene shared this online:

> By talking too much in a meeting or in any kind of situation you make people inadvertently smell weakness on you. A lot of communication between humans is non verbal. We feel, we sense something from you, and it communicates, and we have an impression. And people who talk a lot generally give an impression of they don't know how to control themself. Whereas people who say a bit less…give off an impression of power, as if they know more than they actually do.[4]

Excessive talking is one of the most common areas sales reps struggle with, especially during pricing conversations or when booking trial install dates. Whether it's nerves or lack of understanding the power of being succinct, reps can literally talk their customers into no action.

---

[4] Robert Green, "Speaking Less Will Give You More Power," TikTok, https://www .tiktok.com/@robertgreene/video/7163707483477888302?lang=en.

Learn to cut the fluff and the nervousness. Ask one question at a time. Use only what is needed to get the point across. Think about how you can be as sharp and precise as the finest blade when you deliver your message.

4. Eye Contact

Here are a few tips for eye contact.

First and foremost, you want to be able to read the room. This will only happen if your head is up and your focus is on your customer. To get to this point, you need to know your material. If you prepared well, your focus is not on remembering your next word, it's on your customer.

When it comes to eye contact, you want to mirror how your customer engages with his surroundings. If you have someone who holds eye contact most of the time, do that. If you have someone who makes little or intermittent eye contact, follow their lead. This can get complicated in a room full of different personalities, but with your head up and your attention on your customer, it's very doable.

I should also make the point that too many reps plant themselves behind a laptop during the meeting and use it as a crutch because they are nervous. If you aren't presenting, I'd recommend putting away the laptop and using a notepad so you appear more engaged.

5. Entrance and Greeting

Remember the experiment earlier in the chapter where you sat somewhere and just observed people? You were forming instant impressions of people based on all the non-verbal cues they send.

Use the insights to consider what impression you are creating as you walk into a room. This is something you should give extra consideration to for in-person meetings, but it also matters for video calls and phone calls. What is behind you on camera? Are you immediately focused on calls, fully engaged, and not distracted by other notifications?

One thing to be aware of during your entrance and greeting is to make sure everyone is seen and recognized. Greet each person and treat them all with equal respect. This is not only good manners and the right thing to do. If you focus only on who you perceive to be the most powerful in the room, you may find that someone you slighted turns out to be an important player, too.

I also recommend doing your best to mirror the greeting style of your customers. This has become something to be even more sensitive to in the post-COVID era. Pay extra attention to the signals being sent. (Do they prefer a handshake or fist bump or just a smile, nod, and friendly hello?) Whatever your own greeting preferences, commit to not judging your customers for theirs.

Finally, remember to be succinct in your greetings. Don't be awkwardly abrupt about it, but do remember you are there for a meeting and to get things done—as are your customers. I find that some reps force chit-chat at the beginning of a meeting because they think that is what salespeople do. That's just another lame salesperson stereotype; skip it and get down to business.

If there is an organic conversation that arises and the customer continues to engage, that's fine, but remember you are there for a purpose—a goal—and you have limited time to achieve it.

6. Body Language (Mirroring)

Out of the gate, you want to come across as engaged, confident, and open. The easiest way to do this is to stand up straight, smile, and keep your focus on the room. Avoid the shaking foot, crossed arms, or slouching in your chair. Ultimately it's best to match the "tone" of the body language of your customer. Is the feeling in the room laid back, with everyone kind of casually leaning slightly away from the table in a relaxed sitting position? Then give off the same vibes.

Conversely, if the feeling is a bit more intense, with people sitting up straight in a sterner posture, then mirror that same posture back to them. I sometimes find that inexperienced reps make the mistake of thinking of mirroring as some kind of parody, like crossing your legs exactly like the customer or something like that.

Think of it as more giving back the same body vibes and being tuned into the mood of the room as it is reflected in people's posture. In other words, don't overthink it!

One pro-level tip: I generally recommend avoiding sitting directly across the table from power. This can subtly set up a message of direct confrontation. Sit at an angle to the decision maker when possible, and send the message that you are there as a confident helper and ally that can help them meet their goal. This is not something to get hung up on, just something subtle to consider as you get better and better at the art of meetings.

7. Dress/Appearance on Screen

I talked about the importance of a wardrobe that makes you feel confident in meetings. As you prepare for a meeting the night before, get your clothes together and make sure that everything looks great and is clean and ready to go.

As more meetings have migrated online to video calls, keep up your appearance standards. It can be easier to throw on something too casual at home, decide not to put any time into your hair and grooming, or allow yourself to look like you just rolled out of bed. Do not let your appearance standards slip just because it is on camera.

I should also add that never assume that a virtual meeting will be off-camera. Don't be that rep who has the camera off when all the customers have their cameras on. Don't be the rep who is caught off guard and turns on a camera looking like they haven't showered in three days yet want to ask for a million-dollar deal. A good rule is to prepare for and embrace each meeting as if it were going to be in person.

8. Sitting vs. Standing

As a general rule, you will be sitting in a lot of meetings, even when speaking. However, standing can be a great tool for changing the dynamic in a meeting that is going sideways. If you are constantly keeping your radar attuned to your audience, you will notice when they are getting bored, losing interest, or their energy is flagging.

These moments of need may call for standing up. If you have a whiteboard in the room, that is the perfect excuse to stand up and grab back the attention of the room. Ask questions, write down answers, outline next steps—do something at that whiteboard and get the room engaged again. Take control of the room.

9. Timing

I want you to think of timing in terms of the pace of a meeting. What if you went to a theater to see a play that was three acts and the first act was ninety minutes, the second act was five minutes, and the last act was three minutes? Maybe you just saw the work of a unique genius, but it is much more likely that you just saw a very bad play.

Just like a play needs to have a pace and timing that makes sense, so do the meetings you are orchestrating.

If your meeting is an hour, you probably want to budget about five minutes for greeting and a very quick intro of your company. Then about ten minutes for discovery questions. Budget five minutes to go into a little more background of your company. Then spend about twenty minutes on how you can solve the problem. By now you are right around forty to forty-five minutes. If it is an hour meeting, that is about time to start the meeting wrap up (more on wrapping up a meeting with plenty of time in Chapter 8).

All of these are rough estimates and certainly won't apply to every meeting. The key point is that you need to put thought into these timing issues, both when mapping out the meeting beforehand, and when keeping track of the flow during the meeting.

As the sales rep, you have to own the clock and guide your team to a successful landing. Pay attention. Remember to avoid using phones or computers so your customers don't assume you're distracted. A wristwatch is a great option to stay on track.

10. Punctuality

This one is simple: Always be early. If you have an in-person meeting, build in plenty of time for unexpected traffic or trouble finding the office. If it's online, give yourself enough time for software updates to your video conferencing service or other technical issues. You don't want to be three minutes late to a call with a person with power over your deal because your screen was loading. We'll cover this a bit more in the next chapter.

11. Checking In with Your Audience

We can all fall into the trap of focusing on what we want to communicate, instead of what the customer cares about. If you have done your research and did a quality job with discovery questions, what you want to communicate should match what the customer cares about.

However, you still need to check in throughout the meeting for understanding. Particularly as you describe the solution, you need to build in pauses to stop and ask your customer if what you are saying makes sense and is resonating with them. Something as simple as

"John, I heard you say that X is important because of the Y project and you need to do this by Z date to hit a board initiative. Is that accurate? Did I miss anything?"

Also, tune into their facial expressions as you talk. It is a great indication as to whether they are engaged, confused, or bored. If it is the latter two, it is time to ask them more questions to re-engage them and get to the heart of their pain and problem.

12. Pausing for Power

People who cannot stand silence come across as nervous. People who are comfortable with a pause come across as more confident. That may sound a little simplistic, but it is true. You find the same thing in a movie. A pause at just the right moment of the scene can add a lot of power.

Train yourself to be comfortable making a powerful statement and then going silent. This will allow the important thing you just said to sink in. You need to learn the art of being okay with moments of silence. The customer will often fill in the silence and give you an idea of whether you have connected with them or not.

Examples of when to pause for power include just after you have made a bold value statement about your product or after you have outlined pricing.

13. Connecting with Everyone on a Personal Level

Most people who go into sales have a natural affinity for connecting with others. When they ask about a person's family, their hobbies and interests, or their work problems, good salespeople actually care. There is a genuine curiosity and consideration.

If you don't have this naturally, reflect on why. If it is not something you can develop in yourself, I am not sure sales is your calling. If you do have this genuine interest in others, allow it to blossom in meetings and seize opportunities to make personal connections.

It makes the job more satisfying and allows you to better match solutions to needs. A word of caution: never force small talk and keep personal talk within the bounds of the meeting time. Your first job is to focus on the business problem you are there to solve.

14. Infusing Passion into Your Speech

When you think about infusing passion into your speech, do not think of an old-style Shakespearean soliloquy delivered with grand gestures and histrionics.

To infuse passion into your speech means simply to let your inner fire to solve customer problems reveal itself at the appropriate time in meetings. What about your company, your company's products, and its ability to solve customer problems excites you? If you truly locate a customer's problems and pain through the process of meetings and know you can solve them, then you should be excited to help them. Authentically sharing that through your tone, body language, and inflection is contagious.

When you speak, don't be afraid to let that passion come out. People will recognize the authenticity and trust you because of it. Ultimately passion is another great differentiator when selling.

15. A Call to Action and Departing in Style

This topic is so important, it has its own full chapter later in the book.

Those are the fifteen meeting mastery tools. It probably feels like a lot, and it is. My recommendation is to continue to work your way through the book, where many of these concepts will be expanded upon.

Then return to this list as a guide to work on. Maybe you hire a coach (read more on this in Chapter 10) to work on a particular tool from this list. While you are never done learning, if you can gain basic mastery of these fifteen, you will find that you have become a true artist at running a sales meeting.

A PRACTICAL SUGGESTION

Video is truly one of your best friends when it comes to practicing your pitch, using case studies, or explaining the origins of your company. Use video at home, and use it in combination with your colleagues and teammates (If you want to encourage your manager or executive team in this area, point them to my website https://www.techsaleswarrior.com/ for resources.)

When it comes to getting a handle on how you are coming across to others, eliminating verbal and gestural tics, and understanding how to be more efficient with words, there is nothing to match the power of seeing yourself on video.

Now that you understand the basics of your pitch, it is time to get ready to enter the room.

Action Steps for Chapter 3

- As you work toward learning the art of the sales meeting, this is a good chapter to return to again and again. Skim through the fifteen skills to mastering meetings, and choose one to stop on and go deeper. Assess how well you do it, and then ask yourself, "How can I get better at this skill?"

- Memorize your company's standard script. Do not do this so then you can deliver the same speech like a robot at every meeting. Do it so you have mastery of your material, and can choose what to use in any particular meeting.

- Your ability to communicate is about much more than the words you say. All the non-verbal cues you are sending are just as important, so put a lot of effort into getting this right.

- Video is a tremendous aid in seeing how you are coming across to others. Use it and your improvement will speed up.

CHAPTER 4

PREPARING FOR THE STAGE

*"Being relaxed, at peace with
yourself, confident, emotionally neutral,
loose, and free-floating—these are the
keys to successful performance
in almost everything."*

—DR. WAYNE W. DYER

BACKSTAGE BEFORE A LIVE SHOW is one of the craziest places on earth. If you ever want to witness whacky behavior, watch and listen to some actors right before they head on stage or go before a live camera.

If you closed your eyes and listened, you might think you were in some exotic locale deep in the wild jungle, listening to rare animals bellow, squawk, or screech loudly. If you opened your eyes, you might see limbs bent at all sorts of odd angles, people dancing in a manner that could remind you of some kind of strange bird mating ritual, and all kinds of stretched faces, and bodies doing odd shakes and shivers.

You would guess that seeing and hearing all this strangeness might unnerve an observer, but the truth is it was always a joy. You could feel the energy for the opportunity that was about to present itself (getting up on stage). I remember this dynamic as particularly powerful when I found myself backstage as a guest during *Saturday Night Live*. Because the show was not only live on stage but beamed to millions through television, the energy was completely electric. The higher the stakes, the more intense the magic.

There are good lessons here for anyone who has to stand up in front of others "live." If the thought of conducting your own live meeting makes you nervous, take heart that many actors feel the same as they prepare to shine in the spotlight.

The key to easing the fear is to make a slight alteration in your perception of the situation. Instead of telling yourself you are nervous, remind yourself that this is exciting. Excitement is the positive way of looking at the same emotion that drives your nervousness.

Nervous sounds negative—sweaty, tight, and ready to make a mistake. Instead, say, "Wow, I'm excited. This is going to be awesome because I prepared. I'm going to crush my goal." Making this twist on the same emotion adds a positive spin to the feeling you're going through and calms the nerves a bit before the big moment. This isn't a lie you are telling yourself; you are simply reframing the true emotion in a positive light.

Before you get too concerned, I will not be suggesting barking out guttural sounds or dancing around like a bird before your sales meetings. Extreme warm-ups may be appropriate for actors pumping themselves up for a challenging emotional moment but will not be relevant or helpful to the art of a sales meeting.

However, there are helpful connections between getting ready to perform and how to prepare just before entering a sales meeting.

When an actor is going through their pre-performing ritual, one of the things they are doing is finding a way to transition from ordinary life to the sacred space of the stage. Actors treat their place of performance as an elevated space, which then raises their own performance. Similarly, the best sales reps treat meetings as elevated spaces of complete presence and focus, an idea I will develop more in just a moment.

The other reason actors are so physical and vocal before going on stage is much more practical. It helps to shake out nerves and it warms up your body and your voice. Getting up in front of people always has a physical and vocal component, and you want to already have the energy flowing as you enter the performance space.

This concept of preparing your instrument before the show is rarely discussed in sales training, but it is an important element in every kind of professional performance. The idea of getting warmed up before a meeting gives you a mental edge and a physical sharpness. Top performing actors, musicians, and athletes all prepare in some form to ensure they can maximize their talent in their biggest moments. Why wouldn't you?

Let's look at each of these concepts in turn.

ENTERING AN ELEVATED SPACE

One of my goals in my books is to contribute to ridding the world of the idea of sales as something fake, where the only goal is to trick customers into buying as much as you can sell them.

If you are still early in your sales career, please do not buy into this stereotype in any way; eliminate it. And don't just reject it. Replace it with a vision of yourself as a problem solver, someone who takes away real pain and helps people keep their jobs and advance in their careers.

Meetings give you the best opportunity to fulfill this mission. You will be connecting with people, identifying pain, and detecting solutions. When you have a more pure vision of what it is you do in sales, and you recognize meetings as an elevated space where you can accomplish your mission, you will treat the time in meetings with great respect.

As you think about the tips and methods I'm sharing in this chapter, remember that the goal is to get yourself in that heightened frame of mind and at maximum physical energy so you can raise your game to the level demanded. All of the planning and warm-ups are to prepare you to be fully present in your meetings, so you can give your very best to others.

Of course, given the fast-paced nature of tech sales, it is not always easy to find a lot of time before a meeting to get in the right headspace. What's needed are some simple and effective techniques.

THE FIVE MINUTE QUICK ADJUSTMENT

Whether you've been driving in two hours of traffic or sitting through your seventh meeting of the day, having a way to reset yourself quickly is invaluable. Here are some tips for refreshing yourself and preparing to be in the right mindset for a meeting. Some of them require a private place, so it's not always possible to do all of them before every meeting. Use this any time you feel a little tense, nervous, or just a bit off before joining a phone call or walking into a meeting.

1. **Breathe.** Take five deep breaths in and five deep breaths out. Take five seconds on each inhale and exhale and put all of your attention on your breathing. This is super simple, but it is amazing how calming it is. If you can close your eyes without drawing attention to yourself, then do that. Focus all of your energy on the sound of your breath going in and out. If this leads you to naturally say words of gratitude or a little meditation, go for it.

2. **State the positive reason for your being there.** "I am here to find and potentially solve a problem for [name of client] and will make a dramatic impact for good today."

Or "I am a powerful force for good, and I'm needed in this room today." This is fantastic for a fast refill of your confidence level and a reminder that you have a calling to solve problems for your customers. You may not be able to fix everyone's problem, and you may not have the solution for the exact problem, but you are being called to this moment to potentially help. Affirmations help remind us of that.

3. **Smile, even if you aren't happy.** Physically smiling and holding that face for thirty seconds will impact your mood. Skeptical? Try it. You will feel the difference (there are studies that back this up as well). Depending on how negative your mood is, you may want to hold the smile for an extra minute or two. Do it until your mood improves.

4. **Stretch.** This admittedly is one that can take up a bit more time and requires a bit more privacy. But if you can do this for ten or fifteen minutes, you'll feel more empowered, and your breathing will be steadier and deeper.

5. **Do a quick set of pushups, burpees, or run in place.** Something to get your blood moving and give you an extra shot of energy. If you find yourself with consistent feedback that says something like, "find the passion," "dry," "needs energy," or "boring," this may be a consistent place for you to start before your meetings. Another option is to stomp your feet to ground yourself.

6. **Hum to yourself to warm up your voice, lips, and mouth.** Again, you will want to have a private place, so the client does not think you have lost your marbles. But getting your voice physically prepared gives you more confidence and helps you hit the ground running. If you have the privacy for it, vibrating the lips and speaking vowel sounds will further warm up the instrument that is your voice.

Customize these little pre-meeting habits to the specific situations you find yourself in and to your own personality. But don't skip doing it altogether. You will be surprised how often you will use this and how effective it can be for setting the right emotional and physical state for meetings, be they big or small.

Your own exact "pre-game" ritual will be somewhat unique, and that's, of course, fine. The important idea is to find the best way to get yourself in a state of focus. Not too nervous but still maintaining an energetic edge. Some may rely more on affirmations, and others will put a heavier emphasis on physical preparation.

MEETING PREPARATION: EVERYTHING ELSE YOU NEED TO KNOW

There is no one-size-fits-all checklist I can give you for preparing for a meeting. But here is a fairly comprehensive set of best practices to use for many different kinds of situations.

Leave Earlier Than You Think You Need to Be on Time

There is no worse feeling than scrambling in at the last minute for a meeting. And if you're late, that might cost you the deal. Don't kid yourself, either; some clients can be extremely strict on this.

I remember a large insurance company I was working with in Baltimore. Even though I had prepared my sales team that this particular customer was not okay with folks coming late to meetings (and by late, he meant you should be ten minutes early), the sales engineer joining me that day didn't plan enough time to make it down the busy I-95 interstate. When this engineer showed up ten minutes after the meeting started, the client told the front desk not to let him in the door and that he should leave the premises. Embarrassing, to say the least.

Not having the sales engineer meant not having a complete demo, forcing us to improvise a bit on the fly, and we didn't achieve everything we had set out for with this meeting. Although this example is admittedly a bit extreme, it's important to note that even clients who are not this strict will note lateness, and it may cost you the deal.

Make it a rule to leave with more time than you think you need to get to in-person meetings. You have to expect traffic, getting lost, having trouble finding the office when you get there, canceled catering at the last minute forcing you to find an alternative, realizing you need to stop to pick up a colleague whose rideshare fell through, etc. A hundred potential challenges can present themselves, so leave with plenty of cushion.

For video calls, obey the same principle. You won't have to worry about traffic, but you could run into login problems and other technical issues. Login with plenty of time to spare.

The Night Before

This one is obvious (I hope). Do not go out drinking or staying out late the night before a big meeting. Instead, have a relaxing evening at home. Take time to do some journaling, meditation, and positive affirmations to get in the right mood for a restful night's sleep. Reread the goals of the meeting, review your research, and brush up on your pitch to ensure you know it and are also ready for curveballs that may come at you.

The Morning of a Crucial Meeting

You should already have a positive morning routine as a regular habit. Besides your normal healthy morning, you will want to add the following on meeting days.

Go over the general outline of your schedule for that day soon after waking up. Map out what needs to be done prior to the meeting and plan out when you will accomplish each. Here is a list of what you may need to check or verify:

- If this will be catered, call or stop at the caterer's to confirm timing and that the order is correct.
- If you will be bringing some other kind of treats yourself, do you need to build in time to pick it up? Is there swag

you are bringing from the office, and have you made a plan to get it to the meeting?

- Think through and verify all the tools you will need at the meeting. This includes high-tech and low-tech. Simple things like having your laptop charged and having the right connecting cords with you. On the low-tech side, do you need notebooks, pens, whiteboards, dry-erase markers, or handouts? Create a little checklist, so nothing gets forgotten as you depart for the meeting.

- Also, realize that even though you may have checked as much as you could, technology often still goes wrong. In the thousands of meetings I've been in, the constant is always a non-working projector, a new technology that fails to connect to someone's laptop, a missing cable cord, a screen that won't turn on, etc. Have contingency plans. (More on this later.)

- Ensure everyone on your end who is attending the meeting knows the primary goal of the meeting and their role in the meeting. Plan in advance, so your transitions are natural and smooth.

There's No Such Thing as an Unimportant Meeting

There will be smaller, preliminary phone meetings that don't require extensive checklists. You may tell yourself, "this meeting doesn't count for much," and blow off any kind of preparation. Bad move.

There is no such thing as an unimportant meeting. If it is truly unimportant, why are you even having it? At a minimum, use the five minute reset above to prepare for even the smallest meetings. The more you can be fully present at every meeting, the more you will be ready to seize opportunities when they arise.

Scouting Out the Tech at the Meeting Place and Preparing to Roll with Anything

If you will need tech for your presentation, find out from your customer what will be available to you when it is possible to do so. Get there early to test your tech, including having your PowerPoint presentation loaded up and ready to go.

You also have to know that technical problems will happen, and sometimes there is not a lot you can do about it. One plan should be to have additional equipment (or demos ready, especially if using a cloud) so you can switch screens if the front-line stuff is not working. You should also have a plan for presenting manually if need be.

I remember a meeting where a CIO greeted me at the front desk, and we proceeded to walk through a massive office that seemed to have twenty spacious conference rooms. Yet somehow, we ended up in his office with a small table where we sat two feet away from each other.

A slide presentation or whiteboard was not going to work in this tiny environment. This was going to be an in-depth conversation between two people, and all the hours of prep on the material would have to shine through my words, body language, and presence because I could not rely on the usual technology.

If you are around long enough, these kinds of moments will happen to you in your career. Prepare for the unexpected and be ready to roll with the punches.

A FINAL THOUGHT ABOUT MEETING PREP: BANISH "BAD LUCK"

Most of the things you do the day of the meeting to prepare will focus on making sure that things run smoothly and that things that can derail the meeting are avoided. Some salespeople blame something going wrong on "bad luck." Well, on rare occasions, some truly bad luck can play into it. But the truth is you can outsmart bad luck most of the time with some conscientious planning. Banish the excuse of bad luck from your vocabulary, and focus on what you can control.

You have done all the research, created your pitch, and rehearsed your pitch and stories extensively. You should feel confident and prepared mentally and physically. Now it's finally time to step into the spotlight.

Action Steps for Chapter 4

- Your body and voice are like a tool or an instrument when you are presenting to others. Getting them warmed up before a meeting will sharpen their impact.

- Use the power of the "Five Minute Adjustment" to clear your mind and head into any scenario with more calm and confidence.

- Preparation matters. Little things like setting out your clothes the night before a big meeting can help you avoid problems. And always leave earlier for meetings than you think you need to!

- Treat meetings as an "elevated space." This shows respect to those who you are trying to help in the meeting, and it also honors what you do as a salesperson.

CHAPTER 5

WHAT TO DO IN THE SPOTLIGHT

"Be in the moment. Period. Just be there.
Because if you get all like, 'Oh I got to do this big thing.'
It just never works. It just doesn't work. You've just got
to let go. If it happens, it happens. If it doesn't, it doesn't.
Whatever you do is ok, just be truthful, honest,
real, and that's all you can ask for."

—ROBERT DE NIRO

I HAD MY OWN STAR CHAIR and my own trailer. At moments during the experience, I simply thought, "This is crazy!"

The chair and the trailer were the perks of scoring a role on the long-running network drama, *Criminal Minds*. At one point, I found myself being driven to the set and, amiably chatting with Shemar Moore, the lead of the show.

I'm not going to pretend I was completely immune to getting a taste of the star treatment. It was a small but meaningful reward for all the hard work and rejection that goes along with the life of an actor. Although I had agents and managers, I found and landed this credited role on a major television show through my own networking efforts with casting directors, which made it that much sweeter.

But I don't want you to get the idea that this was all about the flashiness for me. Cool as this was, in the end, I was there to do my job, which was to perform my role to the limits of my ability and training. And to do it on time, practiced, and with flexibility for the situation as the director or other players in the scene may need. When you get a great opportunity, there is no better feeling than rising to the challenge. In short: it is about being a professional.

I find the best sales reps have a similar attitude toward success. The money, perks, president's club trips, and accolades that come along with being successful in tech sales are fantastic. But all those things are a little like a chair with your name on it or chatting with an acting superstar. It's great, but not the main point.

The reps with the most sustained success get the most satisfaction from being great at what they do, continually finding ways to improve, and solving problems for their customers. The journey of getting better at your craft, consistently hitting quota, and successfully achieving customer project goals on time is the true reward that will sustain you over a long career.

That's the kind of feeling I had that day on that set: ready to do my job and confident that I had the skills and preparation to do it.

But then something happened to ratchet up the pressure and create a little more drama than I bargained for.

I played Joshua Sanderson, the "long lost son" of a doctor. My dad was played by Kyle Secor. The doctor had been in prison after being convicted of killing his family; I was the only one among his wife and children who had survived. For the twenty-five years he had been in prison, my character had never seen his doctor dad. During the course of the show, my on-screen dad was proven to be innocent of the killings. Now my big scene, and the culmination of the episode, was to have an emotional reunion with him after his name had been cleared.

The scene was to begin with a driver bringing me to a grassy park where my father was waiting to meet me. When we arrived, the driver in the scene pulled into the wrong spot, and that caused all hell to break loose. This one seemingly small error threw off the filming, and everything ground to an immediate halt.

The director was fuming. He sent the driver away, along with his first assistant director (who was lying in the trunk giving directions to the driver), and called on someone else to drive me for the next take. You might be wondering why this was such a big deal. Was this director just some kind of control freak who couldn't forgive a mistake? Couldn't he have just asked that the driver hit the mark on the next take?

To understand why the director was so upset, it helps to know a little bit about the realities of network television shows. These shows employ large numbers of well-paid, unionized employees, and so the common expression "time is money" is literally true on the set. A screw-up on even a shorter scene can cost a lot of time, and that can mean tens of thousands of dollars get wasted. These kinds of mistakes just can't happen if a show wants to stay within budget. Many television shows give actors one or two takes max per scene to ensure they stay on time and on budget.

So now the director came up to me and said, "Chris, I know it wasn't your mistake, but now we have no margin for error. I need you to get out of the vehicle, hit your own mark in the scene, and nail your part the first time. We cannot afford anything else to go wrong."

Okay, so no pressure or anything! My first big network gig on the most watched show on television at the time—and it has to be perfect in one take.

Adding to my nerves was the nature of the scene. It involved me exiting a vehicle and walking across about forty yards of open ground to meet my "dad" in a park. Covering that distance across a grassy area and nailing your mark exactly is an actor's nightmare. The common mark to hit in a scene is usually only a few feet, not forty yards. So all I had to do was not miss my hugely difficult mark, nail my lines, and convey the exact right emotions in a highly-charged reunion scene while a camera on a crane whizzed into position to capture the perfect final frame of the show. Oh, and please a director who was already highly irritated by what had just happened on his set.

I started getting worked up with anxiety. I looked around and saw dozens of crew members on set, the three cameras focused on my mark, and the stars and hundreds of bystanders. Given the popularity of the show, I knew countless television viewers would eventually see this, too. It seemed a tall order, and I started to think it might be too overwhelming to handle.

But then, just before the scene was set to begin, I was able to draw on something inside myself that allowed me to let my worries go. I was still a little nervous, of course, but I reminded myself that I had trained as an actor for years and that I had the tools and skills I needed to pull this off. It was time to turn nervousness into excitement. I had worked extremely hard to prepare for this particular role and scene, and I was going to make that pay off in the moment.

Because of that preparation, I knew my goal in the scene. I knew I was working with other professionals who would know what the goal was, too. I also knew that if I focused on my intention and the other people in the scene, that would take up all my attention and leave no room for fixating on my nerves. In short, I knew it was time to rely on my skills and preparation as an actor.

This story would end with a bit of an unexpected twist, one I will share with you later in the chapter. Before we get to that, though, let's look at what lessons there might be for a sales rep going into their own pressure cooker of a meeting.

After all, you will be faced with your own challenges being in the spotlight, sometimes in front of a CEO, General Counsel, CIO, CMO, CRO, or CISO who is going to demand as much of you as that director needed from me. And just like my director, that C suite executive will expect you to maximize their time.

HOW TO KEEP YOUR NERVES IN CHECK
AND "HIT YOUR MARKS"

Here is the most valuable advice I can give you to keep yourself on track in any meeting situation: always remember the goal of your meeting. Sometimes you will have multiple goals, but I will refer to this as singular for simplicity and because there is typically one overriding goal.

The power of this advice is that it forces you to keep the concentration away from your own self and all your worries and nerves. Instead, the focus becomes the goal for your meeting—what you can do for others.

Making the goal your North Star as you work through the meeting has benefits that go well beyond keeping you calm and lessening nerves. The customer will notice that you are providing value because you are eliminating extraneous time wasters and concentrating on moving things forward in a methodical way to get their problem solved.

Having a clear goal for the meeting and keeping it top of mind in the meeting is also hugely beneficial if you have multiple people from your own company involved. The goal serves as something to keep the whole team on the same page and provides a benchmark that everyone can use as the measure of success for the meeting.

For example, do not let your sales engineer start showing a demo for the sake of showing a demo. The goal needs to be clear: to tailor a demo to match the specific questions this unique prospect has or lead them to new areas of consideration to solve that problem in a way they never imagined. As sellers, we need to own the planning and guide our technical teams to be as impactful as they can in meetings.

I cannot emphasize this enough, and it is one of the most important pieces of advice in the book: **remind yourself of the goal of the meeting just before entering the spotlight and then ensure that everyone on your team is working towards the same goal**. It needs to be top of mind for all concerned throughout the entire meeting. If you start feeling nervous or lost in the meeting, gather yourself by recentering on the goal.

START WITH QUESTIONS

In Chapter 3, I talked about planning for being in the spotlight and reflecting on what you already know about the customer to formulate some questions to discover more. After greetings and an extremely short introduction, it is to those questions you want to turn.

Don't get lost in small talk or faking familiarity; it only kills precious time and starts the meeting off awkwardly. It can also go completely the opposite of your intent. I once shadowed a sales rep who began the call with a CISO by saying, "You know Ryan, in my research, I see you went to 'X' University. What a shame—always losing."

Everything went completely silent, and it was one of the most memorably awkward meeting openings I have ever witnessed. Of course, the sales rep was actually trying to connect with the CISO with some ribbing (the rep had gone to a competing university). But the delivery—especially without any prior rapport building—created a horrible start.

And, in this case, there was no recovery. The rep fumbled with words as he tried to get back on solid ground, and the tension did not relent. The CISO was offended, never answered any questions on the call, and two years later, had still not bought a single thing from him. Don't overreach and try to force familiarity; focus on your goal and get to the business of questions.

Ask great questions, and you will usually receive great answers. And excellent questions are ones you have put thought into and have purpose behind them.

Bad questions without purpose can derail an entire meeting. Instead of forward momentum, aimless questions create obstacles, waste precious time, and can even backfire and anger your customer. This will make you look amateurish, kill your credibility, and leave everyone more confused than when the meeting started.

Something I shared in my first book, *The Tech Sales Warrior,* can help you get in the right mindset. There I introduced the idea of thinking of yourself as a doctor or detective during meetings. Doctors look for pain and symptoms that reveal root causes that they can treat to solve patient problems. Similarly, a detective questions witnesses and looks for clues that allow them to put together a complete picture of the puzzle they need to solve.

Taking on the mindset of these personas—particularly at the beginning of a meeting—can help you discover how your

Even if the customer's problem may be all over the headlines, you don't want to lead off the meeting with "I know why we are here." Let your prospective customer tell you.

This is even more true if the information is not public and was shared with you by the reseller. Always let your prospective customer be the one to share it, under-skilled questioning by you.

To return to our scenario, here is how you can proceed with the meeting with the CISO.

First, confirm the amount of time you have together and the goal for the meeting. "I just want to confirm, we have forty-five minutes together, and our goal is to understand how to better protect your client's data and to offer your clients more assurance that you are protecting their data across their 365, Salesforce, Jira, and AWS S3 environments?"

Once you confirm agreement on the time and the goal, you have done something really important. You have established a common foundation and set agreed-upon parameters for the meeting. Within those parameters, you can then go to work.

Now move to permission questions. "Do you mind if I ask a couple of questions so I can make this meeting as relevant as possible for you?" The CISO agrees. This, again is a small but important step to make the client feel comfortable opening up to you. You also now have their permission.

As another quick aside, I would like to point out that by establishing the baseline and parameters of the meeting and by asking permission to dig deeper with questions, you are now ahead of

90 percent of sales reps. Most of them will simply walk into a room and start pitching their product. You, on the other hand, are laying the groundwork for a long-term relationship because you are starting off in discovery mode and identifying a company match first.

Your first question about the substance of the problem should be open-ended to allow the customer to tell you about it in their own words.

"Brenda, you mentioned securing your data is important to the firm. Can you share a bit more on what that looks like to you?"

Brenda responds, "Yes, despite having many great tools that we spend millions each year on, we recently identified we were not able to determine who has access to data on a case."

"Oh, wow. That sounds like a very important issue for your firm and your clients. Is that true?"

Brenda again: "Yes, it is. The reason I'm here is we just lost a client that spends a great deal of money annually with us, and I need a plan to fix it, or it's my head."

"I can tell this is very important for you. I want to make sure I have a complete understanding of this issue and the level of urgency. Is there anything else around this issue that you are hoping to achieve besides who has access to your data, and is there a deadline when this project needs to be accomplished by?"

Brenda: "I was telling John [the reselling partner in the room with you] that we need to get something in place this month. This is a massive problem, and between us, the firm is scared we are going to lose more clients because of what just happened. To give you a succinct answer to your question, we needed this yesterday."

"I hear you, and it sounds like because of the severity, the firm has already allocated a budget for this project due to the bottom-line impact?"

Brenda responds: "If we can fix this problem, I can get the money needed. Our attorneys bill one thousand an hour on average, so money is not the issue. I'm more concerned about the time it will take to solve this and if I will still have a job in three months."

Let's pause here and make an observation. Remember, this is the beginning of the meeting, and not once in the entire time have I interrupted with anything about how great my company or product is. That is not the place to start.

Instead, I am simply learning more about this firm, their needs, their pains, the personal and professional motivations, timing, potential budget, etc. This is the value of the doctor or detective persona: seeking answers, and diving deeper.

Imagine if you went to a doctor for the first time, and they immediately launched into their medical school background, why they decided to become a doctor, the history of their practice, and how many patients they served last year. "Okay, that's great, doctor, but I came to see if you could help me with this pain in my knee."

Your job is to focus on your customer's problem first. Draw conclusions and present solutions later. Discovery is best when it comes out of natural, human discussion. No pushing, just trying to understand the problem.

Notice also that if I would have shut down discovery after Brenda's first statement, look how much knowledge I would have missed. I would have missed the crucial detail of just how urgent this is. She needs it "yesterday," and I also learned that she can get the budget because of how crucial this is to the firm.

Knowing all this allows me to reach for a higher goal. Given what I have learned in discovery, I have established timing and budget. It is time to adjust the goal to go for locking in a trial.

At this point in the conversation, you're likely about fifteen minutes into your meeting. You could spend another few minutes uncovering more pain and more budget, but eventually, you need to talk solutions and locking in a trial.

"Brenda, it's clear this problem of not being able to see who has access to data is impacting the firm's ability to retain clients, and it's of major importance for you personally and for the firm. Do you want to trial a product before buying, or would a tailored demo be enough to move forward?"

Brenda: "This is too big of a problem to have something go wrong. I definitely want to ensure it works before buying, or else I will definitely be out of a job, and my credibility in the industry will be shot."

"Understood, so a trial is what works for you. I know this is really important for you, and solving this problem is something I've personally done for dozens of clients in your industry. Given how important this is, I can rearrange a few things on our schedule. Would 2:00 p.m. tomorrow for the install work for your team?"

Brenda: "I'd like to see the functionality real quick in a live demo, but if it looks good, then yes, let's book it."

That's the perfect result for this meeting. Do not start talking too much and confuse things. Simply shift the meeting to facilitating your team's sales engineer, showing only what is relevant to resolving this customer's pain. There's no need for a general product demo or some random cool feature that isn't related to the pain. Stay focused on specifically addressing your customer's problem. Give them just enough to satisfy their need and then you confirm the trial tomorrow and close the meeting.

That was an idealized and necessarily abbreviated example, but I do think it gets to the heart of what you want to do in the spotlight. In a way, what you are really doing is keeping the spotlight off of you and on the customer, their pain, and their problem. That's why you are there, not to aggrandize yourself.

Of course, in some meetings, you may start with lower titles, and your goal is simply to get the next meeting with decision-makers. This same discovery framework is still extremely relevant for those types of situations.

I want to hand you two more tools for great discovery. These are two phrases that are pure gold because they get your prospective customers talking about the right things:

"That's interesting. Can you tell me more?"

"That sounds frustrating. Why is solving that frustration important to the company?"

Super simple, but both give a quick validation of what was just said, and then follow it up with an open-ended question to get your prospect to share in their own words. It is important to remind yourself that your questions must come from an authentic place. If you simply take the questions above, ask them, don't mean it, and try to "game" the meeting or cynically use the emotions tied to an embarrassing company incident, your prospects will smell the fakeness a mile away. You have to be genuinely curious, interested and care about helping your prospective customer.

In an article for *Sandler*, Jonathan Farrington reinforces the importance of genuine questions:

> Effective questioning strategies…will give you a much clearer picture of what the other person feels, believes, wants to know, or understands. This is the secret to positioning yourself and your organization as a trusted resource: being genuinely curious about the other person's world…qualifying the opportunity…and then and only then leveraging your organization's experience and resources to create a customized solution for the problem you've uncovered.[5]

---

[5] Jonathan Farrington, "How to Use Different Kinds of Questions to Improve Your Selling," *Sandler* (blog), accessed February 2, 2023, https://www.sandler.com/blog/how-use-different-kinds-questions-improve-your-selling/.

SOME OTHER KEY REMINDERS WHEN IN THE THICK OF A MEETING

Active Listening/Check-In for Feedback

I have made it clear how much I believe in research and preparation before going into a meeting. However, there is a danger if you go in too sure that you know the problem and the solution ahead of time.

You might begin to hear every customer answer through the filter of your preconceptions that were formed in your research. You have to guard against this by carefully attending to what your customer says. Practice active listening by shutting off your own chatter in your head and fully concentrating on what your prospect is communicating.

Similarly, when it comes time to explain your solution, you can get caught up in what you want to say and forget to check in with your prospect frequently to make sure that your communication is hitting home. Occasionally pausing to say things like, "Does that make sense?" or "How does that sound to you?"

Repeating what you heard and then confirming back is another great tool to ensure you are aligned. "If I heard you right, Sarah, your main concern is replacing your endpoint provider by May 1st, and the solution must come with a managed service since your team isn't big enough to handle alerts? Was there anything else that I missed?"

Rely on Preparation, But Let Pain Be Your Guide

Related to this is that you always want to be prepared to be guided to new insights during a meeting. Do not rigidly stick to a plan you had coming in when you discover that the customer's pain is taking you in a different direction. The actor Alan Alda has summed this up well: "Listening is being able to be changed by the other person."

Alter your plan, or even tear it up and make a new one if the customer problem shows you a better way. Remember, it is always about your customer—not you, not your company, and not your plan.

A good example of altering the plan is what happened in the scenario above. Brenda revealed just how urgent the need was, and the goal shifted to locking in a trial the very next day. Be guided by the pain.

This is why we need to have our pitch material and case studies "off book" (which is acting lingo for having the script memorized). When you do, you can shift with ease as new plans arise in the middle of the meeting. If we don't know our material front and back, the tendency is to rigidly stick to a slide order or canned pitch script that doesn't make sense for this prospect's needs. Sometimes you need to just stop the slides altogether when the prospect is demonstrating they simply want to have a conversation. Real conversations, the ones we all want, may send you in productive directions you never expected. Know your stuff, and then you can remain fully present and able to respond to the flow of the meeting.

Stop Telling People You're Sorry

I have seen something so common in meetings, particularly in young reps, that I have to call it out in a special way here. It's the habit of saying "I'm sorry" during a presentation for a minor slip-up.

First of all, nobody cares about a minor gaffe. Even more to the point, I guarantee most of the time, they don't even know you said something you didn't mean to.

You may know you skipped something in your pitch, or that you said something out of the order you intended, but just smoothly go back and make the point you missed or quickly clarify something you misspoke about. There is no reason to come across as fumbling and apologetic.

If you have ever been to a live theater show where someone has flubbed a line, you probably noted that everyone on stage—including the actor who made the mistake—just keeps going on as if nothing ever happened, and it is quickly forgotten as everyone gets swept back into the action unfolding in front of them. On an equity stage full of proven professionals, you'll likely never even notice such an error.

You need to think the same way. There's no reason for you to say sorry for missing a line. It just brings attention to you, when the focus should be on the action, which in the case of the sales meeting is the focus on solving your customer's problem.

So stop saying sorry! (I should add that, obviously, if you do something worth apologizing for—like, I don't know—knocking over the water pitcher onto the lap of the CEO, then go ahead and say you are sorry. Just stop doing it for every little thing.)

Body Language: Are You Moving Too Much?

I was associated for a brief but wonderful time with the famous Ensemble Studio Theater in New York City. At the time, it was run by the legendary Curt Dempster, who left us in 2007. Curt's reputation for being a true visionary and for mentoring actors was well-earned. I experienced this personally when he one time asked me a simple question that altered my acting and has served me well in meetings, too.

I had just left the stage rehearsal of a play, and Curt came up to me and asked, "Why are you moving so much?"

He was teaching me that every movement is magnified when you are on stage and that my lack of awareness of that fact was hurting my acting. What might be normal movement in everyday life was distracting on stage.

This is just like being efficient with words, only this time with the body. I needed to become more economical with my movements and not be afraid to rest in stillness at certain points of my performance.

This wisdom has continued to serve me extremely well in meetings. You are not performing like an actor, but the dynamic is similar in meetings because all eyes are on you.

Most reps put no thought at all into what their movements are conveying and therefore don't control them at all. But I also see some reps who think they need to make exaggerated movements in order to hold attention.

Actually, the opposite is true. Move with more economy, and you will come across as more powerful. Just like you want to be economical with words, you want to be more efficient with movement.

I also encourage you to bring a stillness to some points of your presentation. There is power in it. This can be combined with "pausing for power" in your speech to communicate a particularly important point. This is the point the great Morgan Freeman was making when he said, "It's what I learn from the great actors I work with: Stillness. That's all and that's the hardest thing."

When you master stillness and economy of movement, your presence in meetings becomes more compelling to others.

Don't "Trash" the Competition; Instead Logically Show Why Your Solution Is Better

As you guide your prospective customer to a solution, it will be natural to want to distinguish your solution from any competition you may have. That is good, but you want to do it in the right way. The wrong way is to think you have to "trash the competition" or even to just subtly put them down.

Take a different approach. First, roadblock your competition by creating an alignment between your customer's goals and your solution—and only your solution—as early as you can in the process.

Second, rather than naming competition, logically map out deficiencies that other products fail to solve but that your product does. In this way, you efficiently define success criteria to battle any future threats before they can take hold.

Do Exactly as Promised

Anytime a potential customer agrees to a meeting, you are essentially promising them something in return: that you will not waste their time.

And that promise involves two components:

One, that you will stick to the time agreed upon for the meeting. This means you need to start wrap-up with plenty of time to smoothly end the meeting on time. Chapter 8 will give you tips and strategies for this.

Two, you are promising to not waste their time by having a clear goal, and that you will have the skill, energy, and organization to stay on track in meeting that goal. So as the meeting draws to a close, bring everything back to confirming the goal was met, and what needs to come next.

This brings it full circle. When you are in the spotlight of a meeting, the beginning and end always come down to the goal for the meeting. Use this as your framework, and you will always be able to "nail your marks" and execute at a very high level.

Speaking of full circle, I should finish my story from the opening of the chapter about the *Criminal Minds* scene. In the end, I was able to hit that mark from forty yards away, and the scene went flawlessly in one take. I hugged it out with my long-lost dad Kyle Secor, and the director was thrilled there would be no more costly delays.

It was a satisfying moment when the director came up afterward and complimented me. He did have a kicker, though. "You know, some of the best scenes in movies and television involve no dialogue."

It was his way of breaking it to me that while my scene would stay, the episode was over its allotted time and the part of the scene with dialogue would be cut. Of course, that was disappointing, but measured against the success of the scene and demonstrating that I could play at the high level of a major network drama, it was still an extremely satisfying moment.

It felt in its own way like a reward and validation for all the training, hustle, and hard work that got me to that point. It felt like there was some magic in it, which is where we go next.

Action Steps for Chapter 5

- All throughout the meeting, remember your goal for the meeting. If you start getting nervous or off-track in any way, redirect your focus back on the goal and off your own worries.

- Starting off with good questions (grounded in research) is much more effective than beginning with a boilerplate pitch. Focus on discovery questions, uncover pain, and then follow it.

- Listen actively and check-in frequently for feedback. This is not a lecture, it is a conversation.

- Mind your body and avoid the common error of being fidgety. Work on stillness and calm.

- It's always about the goal for the meeting. Keep yourself and your team focused on that.

CHAPTER 6

THE MAGIC OF DISCOVERY

"But one of the things I learned from improvising is that all of life is improvisation, whether you like it or not. Some of the greatest scientific discoveries of the 20th century came out of people dropping things."

—ALAN ARKIN

THERE'S A MEMORABLE SCENE in Martin Scorsese's 2013 film *The Wolf of Wall Street* with Leonardo DiCaprio and Matthew McConaughey. The characters they play are having lunch, and at one point McConaughey begins pounding rhythmically on his own chest during the meal. If you have seen the movie, you remember it because it turns into one of the most dynamic scenes in the film.

What many people don't know about that scene is that McConaughey's chest-thumping was not planned and wasn't even in the scene until around the sixth take. It was a technique that McConaughey had used for years to calm himself and get out of his own head before doing takes throughout his career.

DiCaprio asked McConaughey to bring the chest-thumping into the scene, and he agreed. The result of that simple "yes," just being willing to take a small step in a different direction, generated magic that freed the two personalities to leap off the screen.

Another even more iconic moment in another Scorsese film came when Robert DeNiro looked in the mirror and said, "You talkin' to me?" This scene from *Taxi Driver* was entirely made up in the moment. DeNiro has had a career full of memorable lines, but this is probably his best-known line, and it was completely improvised.

Other times, spontaneity can seem to go bad, only to turn out well. I remember in one of my early scene study classes, I was performing in a John Patrick Shanley play. The scene was serious and full of heightened emotion. The moment called for me to blow out a candle, which I did.

The wax from the candle shot back in my face. The serious spell was broken, and the audience laughed as I battled to see through the wax on my face. In almost instantaneous succession, it was scary, then embarrassing, then hilarious. It opened up a whole new dimension to the scene not written on paper, and the audience went wild. As the saying goes, the show must go on. And sometimes that is a good thing.

I want to make the case in this chapter that sales has its magic moments, too. It might not quite reach the level of the thrill of winning a Super Bowl, or landing a Tony, Emmy, or Oscar, but it can deliver up moments where you are completely present, fully alive, and helping people reach their goals. And that mindset of magic can be tremendously satisfying and keep you from burning out or falling into the trap of seeing your job as only a way to make money.

What are the keys to finding this magic in tech sales? The key is shifting to the mindset secret of improv players, known as "Yes, and..."

THE MAGIC OF IMPROV

During my acting career I had some great experiences with well-known improv groups like Upright Citizens Brigade, The Groundlings, and Second City Chicago. It truly was an amazing education. As a direct result of what I learned, I booked several national commercials and, ultimately, a pilot with Ashton Kutcher's team, the people behind the show *Punk'd*.

Improv can be a little scary but also incredibly fun. Learning to turn fear into excitement and creativity is one of the best skills you can learn. It will give you the confidence to feel you can rise to meet the challenge of any new opportunities that arise.

But how do you learn to turn fear into excitement and magic?

It comes down to discovering the power of "Yes, and..."

Improv can take many forms. You might start with the shout-out of a single word from the audience. Or it can start with a character or situation—anything that could be taken in a million different directions. Essentially, you are creating something out of almost nothing and doing it on the spot.

The only way to build something out of thin air starting from zero is to take everything that is said and then think, "Yes, I agree and accept that (no matter how outrageous). And now I am going to add something to build on the story and create new connections."

This way of thinking teaches you that for magic to happen, you need to start with the positivity of a yes, and then add your own value to the conversation. If someone negatively rejects the previous statement, it stops the building of something potentially great in its tracks.

You also learn that it is essential that everyone adds value, including yourself. You absolutely must rely on and listen to others, because otherwise you will become lost. But that also means your scene partners are counting on you. Everyone has to be present and in the moment for the best improv experiences.

Improv definitely cures you of the bad habit of thinking of what you want to say before the other person is done speaking. You are forced to listen fully because you need to build on it and if you miss what is said, the moment passes you by.

My favorite improv experience was when a group I was a part of won the championship in an Upright Citizens Brigade sketch contest. Sketch is more of a character-based form of improv instead of ideas being shouted out from the crowd. In this case, we had eight guys playing early American history legends. The premise we came up with was a Founding Fathers' holiday party at James Madison's house. As the sketch played out, we learned that the shrimp soup was causing food poisoning. As you might imagine, if you put eight guys together with this kind of premise, it can get pretty crazy fast.

The dignity and seriousness with which we are used to talking about the Founding Fathers versus the all too human problems associated with food poisoning made for some great moments. But a promising premise is never enough with improv. The keys are that everyone has to buy into what the others say, stay present in the moment, and then jump in with their own value. I remember that experience as one of the most alive and present moments with another group of people in my life.

What can we learn in sales from improv and the philosophy of "Yes, and…"?

I believe there are three key lessons.

One is to stay positive, listen carefully, and then add your own value. You will learn to stay more open during the discovery phase, and you will also be ready to change to meet the needs of your customer.

Two is to be willing to roll with what happens. This is easier the more you become a master of meeting skills. You will have enough confidence that the unexpected will no longer be something you fear, but instead be a challenge that excites you.

Three, your customer's responses will now become driving forces that you can build upon. Each meeting becomes unique, unexpected, and exciting. The problems you identify, the pains, the fixes are all new. You'll go on new adventures, down unknown paths. You'll feel alive.

Here are three times when moments turned magical, through hard work and staying in a "Yes" frame of mind.

Moment One

In my early days as a cold calling TDR/BDR/SDR, I cold called a SLED account and gave a very specific pitch. I really leaned in and began with the pains our product solved.

The CISO on the other end of the line finally spoke. "Is this a joke?"

Baffled for a second, I didn't let it throw me. "No, I'm dead serious. What do you think about booking a meeting on Friday at 2:00 p.m.?"

There was a silent pause. "Either someone clued you into our current project needs or it's your lucky day, because this is exactly what we need to solve in the next month, and I need pricing today."

Within three weeks my SR closed a $180,000 deal that started with that cold call.

Moment Two

A partner had set a meeting for me with a regional healthcare system a few hours outside Washington DC. They were a regional powerhouse but didn't get much love or facetime from the vendor OEMs because it took effort (hours of driving) to get there, and there was nothing fun to do around the city (unless you liked hiking in coal country).

When we started the meeting, the CIO was a bit standoffish and dismissive. He and his team voiced objections, and we actively listened and told them specifically how we solved each one.

We also boldly said we could solve all of them in three weeks or less during a free POC. The CIO scoffed.

I stayed fully present and confidently told him the truth. "We've done this exact same thing for hundreds of companies including the XYZ healthcare firm an hour away."

The company was still unconvinced but starting to see that we were problem solvers. The CIO chimed in, "We hear a lot of things from salespeople. I've got to see it to believe it."

"No problem," I said, and then in the moment decided to say, "But if we do prove it out as we just discussed, since this is the exact solution you need, do I have your commitment to move forward with an order in thirty days?"

"We'll need to work out numbers, but if so, then yes," the CIO said. "But I still don't believe it." The magical word yes was enough, and forty-five days later, the deal was in the books. Another two hundred and fifty grand closed, and a new logo in the books.

Moment Three

During discovery with a large credit union, we found out that they were on the brink of missing an audit point that would impact their standing with the National Credit Union Administration.

This was a career-defining moment for the credit union's CISO. If he turned this around and nailed the audit point in time, it would mean a nice bonus. If he missed it, the organization would lose its accreditation, and he would have been fired by the union's board.

This is exactly why you do discovery, to find that magic intersection of personal pain, company problem, and your solution. Because we uncovered exactly what needed to be done and the personal urgency, we were able to be crystal clear on exactly what we could and could not achieve in thirty days.

Not only did we receive a $300,000 order, but because we followed through and delivered on what we promised, the CISO became an amazing referral machine for us.

He benefited greatly from solving the credit union's problem, and we did well in return. Finding these lifelong, symbiotic relationships are game changers and definitely possible when you discover the intersection of company impact and personal impact, and then explain clearly what you can do to help. Of course, above all, you stick to your word and overdeliver on the promises you make.

The improv mindset also keeps you from getting locked into your own preconceptions and makes you more nimble. I remember one improv show where a scene partner started by moving their hands around in a big circle and I started thinking, "Oh, it's a wheel, we're about to start talking bicycles."

Then he says, "Wow, remember how mom always used to make us churn milk into butter in the morning." Whoa, okay, forget bikes,

I have to work off of butter now! There's nothing to do but say yes to the premise and then think of your own, "And…"

None of your prospective customers are likely to start talking about butter churning, but they will come out with things you do not expect. Will you be ready with a "Yes, and…"?

Where You Can Learn More about Improv Skills

If you live in or near New York, Los Angeles, Toronto, or Chicago, finding a world-class improv show to attend will not be hard. The Groundlings, The Second City, and Upright Citizens Brigade are three of the biggest names, but there are plenty of others in these cities. In addition, other cities across the US will have opportunities to see improv, and there are improv spots on or around many colleges. In short, you can almost for sure find a show if you want to see one.

If you go, I recommend thoroughly enjoying it, but also doing some analysis of what you are seeing. Observe how the players pull off the "Yes, and…" technique. When something does not work as well, or even crashes and burns, why? And how did the players handle it? Sometimes thinking about the mechanics and craft of improv is as much fun as the show itself. You are also learning lessons to help you when presenting.

If you want to go deeper, look for theaters or improv companies that offer training. Some organizations even offer classes specifically aimed at non-actors who want these skills for their careers or personal life. If you happen to live in Los Angeles, the Upright Citizens Brigade (the original founders included superstars like Amy Poehler and Adam McKay) offers training and live shows to see long-form improv works in person.

You can also observe and learn about improv without leaving your couch. I highly recommend checking out the show *Middleditch and Schwartz* on Netflix. If you pay attention, you will gain insights into how simple questions, listening, and building on top of small moments can be turned into profound stories.

MAGIC HAPPENS MORE OFTEN WHEN YOU ARE A MASTER OF YOUR CRAFT

One of the things I want to hammer home in this chapter is that there can be more fun, excitement, and tremendous satisfaction in tech sales than many people in our field realize. The key is to learn to be present in the moment and get to the magic. When it happens, it is a success to be savored.

Life is always throwing us curveballs, but when we learn to say "yes, and…" it raises everyone's energy level and elevates the moment. When we listen and lean into these unexpected discoveries, the moment is electrified, and everyone is drawn in.

However, the price of admission to play at this level is not something everyone is willing to pay. What is that price?

It is a matter of dedicating yourself to learning and mastering all the skills that we have covered up to this point in the book. It's being willing to fail at them, to take constructive criticism from managers and team members, and keep moving forward.

If you work hard at these skills, you'll reach a point where you can bring all those skills to be fully present in the moment of the meeting. You can get to that "fully present" state because you have reached a level of mastery that gives you the confidence to be in command of yourself and the meeting.

You will also learn to recognize that fear can be turned into excitement. When you have done this enough times successfully, you no longer have to convince yourself to overcome fear by transforming it with excitement. It will come naturally because you learn to love the excitement of being in the moment.

Being fully present in meetings will also make you a master at honing in precisely on what makes your solution important to them *right now*. You are trying to find out what makes your customer tick on both a personal and professional level.

You'll begin to know that feeling in the meeting when you are getting close to the magic, and you'll keep probing and staying in the moment. Suddenly you'll see the way to map and align your solution to your customer's problem, and be able to communicate it with power, precision, and passion.

When all the tumblers click into place, you'll feel that magic of discovery and realize that your job can be immensely satisfying and rewarding, and not just monetarily.

Believe it or not, some of the most satisfying of these kinds of triumphs are when you initially meet the most resistance. Let's talk about some of the ways you can break through to still find the magic when your prospective customer is not opening up.

WAYS TO UNCOVER PAIN WHEN
YOU MEET RESISTANCE

What happens when you are in a meeting and you cannot seem to break through and get your clients to open up about the problems they need solved?

This is not uncommon. Many times, a prospective customer will be reluctant to talk about the full extent of the problem. After all, sharing pain is—well—painful.

If you look at this from the customer's point of view, you are asking them to tell you about a shortcoming or maybe even a failure in their company's performance. For the people in the room, that can feel very personal. Whether it is a security failure, the servers being down causing everyone in the business to hate IT, or a technology limitation that slows down the efficiency of the business, no one enjoys explaining where their performance is falling short. For those of you selling cybersecurity, it will be especially common for leading firms to push back on sharing pains.

So it goes with the territory that prospects will often feel uncomfortable opening up. Inexperienced reps often react to this awkwardness by retreating into a standard pitch. It feels safer than exploring pain points with the customer.

But you cannot master the art of the sales meeting if you flinch when it is time to go deeper into the problem or run from facing tough conversations. How can you stop yourself from shying away from exploring your customer's pain?

The first thing to think about is whether there is a legitimate barrier to the customer sharing more. Sometimes a company will need a Non-Disclosure Agreement (NDA) in place before sharing details about the problem. NDAs are not always necessary, but if you sell tech products that cover sensitive areas of company business, this can be an issue.

This is something to bring up early in the process, when appropriate, so that when you get to substantive meetings, your customer will be able to share more precise information with you.

However, getting an NDA is not the real challenge. It is only a formal first step. The true task is to fully explore the problem while not putting your customer on the defensive.

If you find yourself shrinking back from going into the pain deeper with your customer, here are some strategies and techniques to get them to open up.

Rely on a More Experienced Team Member

For reps still learning to master the skill of uncovering pain, having seasoned team members in the meeting with you can be invaluable. You need to anticipate when a meeting would benefit from having senior team members involved so a plan can be made to ensure they will be in attendance.

Of course, do not just sit there enjoying them doing the work for you. Observe them closely and learn how they work to skillfully and sincerely uncover pain and problems that need solving. Take extensive notes.

Gauge the Room

Much of this boils down to being fully attentive in meetings. Anyone who makes the effort can generally get a good feel for the level of trust in the room by body language and tone of voice coming from the others in the room.

If things feel tight, go a little slower and explore with special tact. Share case studies or use examples that align with their challenges and how your team has worked with similar firms. If the mood in the room begins to loosen, say just enough to be encouraging. The magic happens when you let prospects share their problems in their own words.

A *Great* Question to Help You in These Situations

If you are starting to feel the trust in the room, but are afraid a very direct question could put the customer back on the defensive, use this question: "Do you mind if I ask you a couple of questions to understand the problem more and make better use of your time today?"

I cannot remember any time in any meeting where I used this question and did not get a positive response. This way of phrasing it shows sincere respect to them because you are asking their permission before going deeper on something that may be painful for them to share.

It also frames the follow-up questions you are about to ask in a positive light. Instead of the next questions coming across as potentially abrupt and intrusive, you are showing them that you are asking questions so you can better understand the problem, which will help you provide a better solution. It's important that the questions that follow are strategic, authentic, and motivated by truly wanting to understand their unique challenges.

Put Yourself in Their Shoes

One of the other ancillary benefits of learning improvisation is that it awakens your imagination to overcome tough challenges and obstacles. Relating to your prospect and the challenges they face is another way to get to know them, their problems, and their daily struggles.

This ultimately flows from how powerful your preparation is and how well you can do when on your feet in the room. Former CRO of Hubspot and author Mark Roberge echoes the need to know and cater to prospects in the *The Sales Acceleration Formula:*

> Salespeople need a high degree of business acumen in order to fully understand their buyers' goals. Salespeople need to transform their product's generic messaging into a customized story that resonates with the buyer, addresses the buyer's needs, and uses the buyer's terminology. The best-trained salespeople have experienced the day-to-day job of their potential customers. This modern form of selling requires the salesperson to truly understand what it's like to be in their customer's shoes. What do they do all day? What is easy about the job? What is hard? What causes stress? What do individuals in this role like to do? What do their bosses want them to do? How is success measured?[6]

---

[6] Mark Roberge, *The Sales Acceleration Formula: Using Data, Technology, and Inbound Selling to Go from $0 to $100 Million* (New York: Wiley, 2015), pg. 60.

If your company has real-world labs that highlight the business problem, I would recommend any seller to get involved to feel the technical pain firsthand of what your solution solves. This additional insight will give you the ability to relate in a technical manner that many of your competitors won't.

Your ability to say an authentic "yes, and…" to customers goes up when you have a better understanding of what their work day looks like. As an actor gets to know a character they are playing, the salesperson should get to know the prospect they are selling to. Find more ways to connect by imaginatively living through the pains they face.

Never Belittle, Use Scare Tactics, or Condescend (Even if You Think You Are Doing It in a "Nice" Way)

I'm guessing that most reps already intuitively know that belittling or condescending to prospective customers is a bad idea. However, make sure that you are not coming across this way unintentionally.

For example, if you sell cybersecurity solutions, you may be tempted to make a company feel bad or guilty about a potential or actual security breach as a way to motivate them into buying. Of course, the risk of their poor security may be very real, but you telling them that directly will likely come across as condescending or manipulative. This will make them less likely to share the full extent of their pain. In the worst cases, they may boot you out and you will have zero chance to do business with them ever again.

Instead, ask them questions and let them tell you what their risks and problems are. Then repeat what they said back to them in their own words to confirm understanding. Using their words and confirming what you heard strengthens trust and likeability in the room.

This could apply to any number of types of tech sales. Maybe a company is not using a product that most of its competitors use already. They are falling behind revenue goals because of it. Trying to shame them for being slow to get on board is the wrong way. Asking questions about how much additional revenue could be added with the right solution is the right way.

BREAKTHROUGH

Magic is not going to happen every day. You can do all the right things, master the right skills, and you are never going to have a 100 percent close rate. Even great improv actors fail miserably from time to time.

But the more you achieve mastery and the more you open yourself up to the magic of staying fully present, the more opportunities and relationships you will find. It will amaze you. These tools help open our minds to new possibilities and new courses of action. The "yes, and…" mentality can also help think creatively about unique events for your region that may help propel new prospects to attend, ultimately driving your pipeline up.

Think of your job as bigger than just you and your salary and your bonus. You are on a mission to solve problems and serve others. Each person and each company will have needs and challenges as unique as a fingerprint. Find that fingerprint, and you will find the magic.

Action Steps for Chapter 6

- Magic happens more and more as your mastery of meeting skills improves and you trust the moment. Use that as motivation and fuel to push yourself to get better.

- As you work on upgrading your skills, remember to rely on trusted team members and don't be afraid to ask for help and guidance.

- Use this great question to set yourself up for success in a meeting: "Do you mind if I ask you a couple of questions to understand the problem more and make better use of your time today?"

- If you truly believe you have a mission to serve each unique customer by potentially solving their pain, you give yourself the gift of great confidence to walk into any unknown. When you find that matching fit between their problem and your solution, and then logically map out the fix, it is a great feeling.

- Embrace the unexpected. The vulnerable moments in a meeting when met with a "Yes, and..." will make all of your meetings more exciting and ultimately lead you to new findings and adventures with your customers that you couldn't have predicted or originally known.

CHAPTER 7

PRICING: A COMMON PERFORMANCE PITFALL

"Know your lines and don't bump into the furniture."

—SPENCER TRACY

AS A KID, I WAS ALWAYS looking for ways to make money. I guess part of this came from wanting to help out our large family—there were five of us kids, and supporting all of us was something my parents had to struggle and work hard to maintain.

Plus, entrepreneurship and business success just naturally fascinated me (and still do). My entrepreneurial ventures as a kid included lawn mowing, snow shoveling, babysitting, and painting. I also ventured into door-to-door selling, hawking holiday gift wrap and chocolates. And then, I embarked on more quirky stuff like holding impromptu yard sales with any donated items I could get my hands on, started book clubs using my parents' books, and held movie nights.

I also tried my hand at that most classic of all kid businesses: the lemonade stand.

My lemonade stand got off to an amazing start. For weeks, my stand had zero competition, and the neighbors were consistent, repeat customers. They were either being nice, or they truly enjoyed it, but the dollars rolled in, and the feedback on the taste was excellent.

Business was good, and the living was easy.

And then another neighborhood kid showed up and had the audacity to set up shop directly across the street. That I now had competition was bad enough, but this smarty pants also slashed his prices. I watched as my customers flowed across the street. My profits took a hit, and so did my ego.

It got worse. Other copycat stands started popping up. Many of these went in and out of business pretty quickly because they seemed to lose interest in the work fast. But still, it all cut into my business, and times were tough after everything had started off so well.

Finally, one afternoon my frustration boiled over, and I furiously stormed into my house.

"What's going on?" my mom asked.

I went into a full rant mode and got a little incoherent.

"They keep dropping the prices, and one of them literally set up their table ten feet from mine!" I said. "John's mom is buying all of their products, and now they have added Kool-Aid to their menu too."

My mom then calmly gave me some great advice that has served me well ever since.

"Chris, this is the American way, and competition is a good thing," she said. "You have to think creatively on how to win."

In the heat of the moment, that was not what I wished to hear. I wanted my mom to indulge me in my pity party and validate my frustration. I ran to my room and sulked for a bit. But self-pity gets boring fast, and then my mom's words came back to me, echoing in my head. "You have to think creatively to win."

Then this weird (but creative) train of thought flowed through my head. I spotted a gold wig in my room. That reminded me of a clown costume in our basement. And then I thought, what do clowns do? They perform for audiences.

An audience. Yes, that's what I needed to differentiate myself. A bigger audience, something to stand out, and a way to draw them in. I thought of the mass of untapped traffic that never came through our neighborhood but did pass by it. I could move my stand to the top of our street to gain more exposure and do something that grabbed their attention. Draw the audience in, and then sell them some lemonade.

Within the hour, I had talked one of my sisters into dressing up in the clown costume, and I slapped that gold wig on my own head.

We moved our stand to the top of the street where the traffic was probably fifty times what went through our neighborhood.

Profits soared, and we had more fun along the way. Our customers enjoyed it, too. We were serving with passion, we had a consistent product, and we made accessing our stand easier. I knew we had hit the big time when one of our parish priests said to my mom, "Did I see your kids in clown costumes selling lemonade on the side of the road?"

Later we added sno-cones and Snapple to the menu, and bigger revenue streams emerged. The other sellers seemed to lose interest, and suddenly all the competition evaporated.

There are two lessons in this simple story that I think are worth bringing out.

As you prepare for your meetings, much of your success will rely on what you do in advance of your meetings—how much you understand your customer's pains and needs, their budget, their economic buyers, and their sign-off processes. It will depend on how creative and passionate you are about what you sell and the impact you have on your customers day to day. It will also be dependent on how much you have differentiated your product's value to their business, and how you take what you have learned to plan for the next meeting or next step in the sales cycle to move the deal along. When you do all these things and add authentic fun along the way, you distinguish yourself from the crowd.

Leave the gold wig and clown outfit at home, but do use your own brain and take my mom's advice: you have to think creatively to win. Many of you in the infrastructure, EDR, and firewall spaces face enormous competition—how will you creatively gain attention? That's the first lesson.

A LESS OBVIOUS LESSON

There's another lesson buried in this story, and it is the one I want to bring out because I think it is actually even more important than the obvious one.

To put it in the simplest way: winning in sales is more than just pricing. Once I had better marketing and differentiation (the clown outfit and gold wig, a better location, and a higher-quality product), pricing became much less of an issue.

Of course, that's not to say that pricing doesn't matter at all. It does. If I had tried to charge $10 a cup for my lemonade, even a carful of clowns wouldn't have saved my business. But what I do want you to understand is there are many areas we can improve beyond our price to win more deals.

Closing a tech sale is more complicated than a kid's lemonade stand. However, we can make the same rookie mistake of putting too much emphasis on price alone. Now that I have been a part of thousands of software deals in my career, I can attest that the vast majority of deals do not require slashing of prices, even in tough economic climates. If you deliver aligned value to your customers and differentiate from the market with clear detail (like product capabilities, superior support, etc.), and you have mapped these to a budget range stated by your economic buyer early in the sales cycle, you will not need to offer significant price reductions to get the sale.

This is not just my own personal career experience. I have seen dozens of sellers on my team prove that price is only one of many factors in closing an enterprise deal.

Yet many reps still get caught up in believing that the secret to negotiation and price agreement is all about dropping the price. It's not. Let's dive into how to tackle pricing in a very practical way.

FIRST, ELIMINATE FEAR

When I made the transition to sales, I recognized how the fears of acting were similar to those of selling. Cold calling is kind of an equivalent to an open audition or a "cold read" (where you are not given a script ahead of time). One of my most memorable cold-read situations happened when I went out for Admiral Kirk in what would be the start of another set of major Star Trek films.

With no script given in advance, I showed up with about thirty minutes to read "the sides" (the name for an audition script). That half hour was all the time allotted to prepare for the rare opportunity for a life-changing role. In those moments, you have to fall back on your training and trust your instinct. There's no time to mull over twenty different approaches to the moment. Part of what you learn is to accept that there's going to be a lot of rejection, understanding that will stir up emotions, and yet still going ahead and giving it your best.

This chance happened somewhat early in my acting career, but

I did have at least a few years under my belt. Although the role eventually went to Chris Pine, I was pleased that I had enough training by then to have competed well for the role under cold audition conditions.

This is the point you want to reach in your sales career. Whether it is thinking on your feet on a cold call or mastering your fear of presenting pricing, the more you push yourself to grow and meet challenges, the better you will become.

For various reasons, pricing is one of the most common areas where sales reps fail to rise to the moment out of fear. It is the equivalent of an actor shying away from taking on the full emotion of a highly impactful moment in their scene.

What does it look like when a rep starts struggling with being forthright about price? Endless speaking in circles about everything but price, followed by lots of apologies before sharing the price. Sometimes a sales rep will shut things down with a preemptive "No, I can't change the price," while they sit there with sweaty hands, darting eyes, and shaking legs. Others cave and try to just give the product away with discount after discount in the hopes a customer may eventually buy.

If you have fear around pricing, you need to work through it. You need to analyze whether you are not bringing some baggage around this issue. One area to consider is how you deal with personal finances. Issues surrounding money are some of the most emotional, and many of us drag things from our childhood experiences into the meeting room.

Looking at your own spending habits on similar-sized purchases (to what you sell) may reveal clues to how you guide buyers to decisions about your product. For instance, if you tend to shop around for many months on a $100,000 purchase, you may lead your customers to do the same. This is not helpful when closing sales efficiently is important for your long-term success.

If you have trouble being direct about money and pricing, you need to do some journaling and reflecting in this area. Sometimes even professional help can assist you if you have particular long-standing struggles in this area.

The other thing you need to question is if you believe strongly enough in the value of what your company and its products bring to others. If what you deliver solves big problems, increases profits, or protects companies from liability, then why be squeamish about asking for a price that reflects the value you bring?

Sales frameworks and methodologies like MEDDPICC and Value Selling focus on the exact point. How do you share the quantifiable value your solution provides? Thinking this way forces you to quantify return on investment or what you are solving in dollar terms for your customer. Does that align with the cost of your solution? Remember, these are the kinds of things you should be seeking out early in the process to further qualify that you have a real opportunity.

Also, remember, saving people's jobs, helping them get promoted, or assisting them in earning bonuses are valuable, too. Why be shy about asking for your price? You provide value, and you should not be reticent about asking for a price that reflects that. A quote from

Warren Buffett sums all this up perfectly: "Price is what you pay. Value is what you get."

In the end, if you fear pricing, it is something you are creating in your own head. Do the personal work to overcome it.

Getting to a yes on price does take a little more nuance than other parts of the sales process, but it is also not nearly as tricky as it is often made out to be. There are five big things to get right when it comes to pricing and meetings. If you nail these, you can master pricing.

THE FIVE THINGS YOU NEED TO GET RIGHT ABOUT PRICING

1. Verify Price and Timing Early and Often and with the Right Person (or Persons)

You should always begin early in the process to validate that the customer's budget is a fit for your product's price range, and then continue to verify that all through subsequent meetings. If you do, pricing fears and issues will evaporate.

This does have a big caveat, however. You need to verify pricing not only early, but with power. Emma Brudner makes this point in an Hubspot.com article, where she says one of those essential skills is speaking with the decision-maker.[7] This fundamental step is

---

[7] Emma Brudger, "12 Essential Negotiation Skills for Salespeople," *HubSpot* (blog), February 2, 2022, https://blog.hubspot.com/sales/essential-negotiation-skills-for -salespeople.

often overlooked or misunderstood. It does get a little complicated at times because sometimes the person you need to align with on the technical side may be different than the person you need to greenlight the budget. You may even have more than two powerful stakeholders in many deals.

You need to figure that out, but whoever has ultimate authority over the budget is always going to be key, and you need to get to them and validate pricing as early as possible. If you are able to do that, why would you be worried about formally presenting the price? You have already laid the groundwork with the person who owns the budget, so the number should not come as a surprise.

Pro tip: Just because they are the C-suite executive doesn't mean they have the power to sign the purchase order. It may be a different executive who has ultimate authority, or for some deals, you may need the CEO. Do not make sloppy assumptions, because each organization is unique.

Whatever the specific situation, if you go to lock in pricing with your customer and they have sticker shock, you skipped a step in the process. This is something you will want to go back and analyze to figure out how you can get it right the next time. Most of the time, you will discover that you should have started talking about pricing earlier, and with the person who had the power.

Back when I was a rep, I remember a terrific pricing call that my boss asked to join. He asked the customer, "Do you think your team will be able to move forward this quarter?" To which my executive sponsor responded, "The PO went out to the partner a moment ago."

This final pricing call lasted about two minutes because all of the steps had already been knocked out. My boss's response? "Wow, well, that was easy. Have a great day." Pricing does not have to be hard when you align with power early and often.

Of course, you need to beware of "gotchas." Actually, you should expect them, because we all operate in a very competitive environment.

Some firms shop prices around to third parties to understand the supposed "industry standard discount or price." This, more often than not, leads to customer confusion when the third party reports back general insights about a software/hardware vendor's pricing, but fails completely to understand the specifics of your deal.

Instead of being frustrated, embrace these situations by being transparent about your discounts and clarifying the discount needed to land the deal. Don't wait for time to solve this because it won't. Confusion will lead to opportunities for competitors.

The sales proverb that "time kills all deals" is true. So take the reins and close this off before you have a runaway pricing situation. Also, think ahead to what your procurement team may need to agree to the price. Prep for those situations, by adding margin into your deal. This is a good reminder that before committing to a deal, find out what may go wrong in the process and be prepared to address it swiftly. Don't get "happy sales ears." Instead, think: "What am I not asking here? What have I missed?" What could go wrong? Why may the deal not come in?

For most of us that live and die by our performance in quarter-year increments, you want to always be proactive with timing. The best approach is to always work off your customer's timelines. What needs to be achieved by x date for them to hit their goals? You can use their goals as a company to work backward from procurement to final meetings to trial to install, etc.

Help your customer to visualize all the steps and the timing by creating a document with all the key milestones and dates along the way. This way, everyone has the same north star to keep things moving in a productive direction. If you find yourself in a situation where you are nearing the end of the quarter, and your customer hasn't met their portion of the deal (meaning the PO hasn't been released), lean on the relationship you have built.

One of my former bosses liked to say, "avoid the scolding parent approach," and lead by asking for a personal favor. Many sales reps are tempted to leverage their anxiety about missing a quarterly goal by sending a nuclear missile—an email threatening a price increase.

A better approach is to connect on a call or in person with your buying champion and share the importance of the deadline. Re-share the document where you have laid out all the key dates that logically allow for all sides to meet the deadline. Then ask for it in the context of a personal favor to get this done. It is crucial to note that this approach only works if you've built rapport with your prospect's team throughout the deal and delivered on all of their success criteria.

2. Why Now?

Back when I was involved with the Ensemble Studio Theatre in New York, one of the directors would always ask, "Why today? What's different? What's so important about now?" It forced you to think about the circumstances, the uniqueness, the importance, and the compelling events surrounding the play.

One of the many joys of our work as sellers is doing great detective work with our clients where we can probe in a similar way. When you do this well over time, you'll notice that although there are similarities in what your solution solves, each client has its own special needs, pains, and professional and personal goals. For example, the selling system taught by Sandler uses the Pain Funnel to teach reps to lower the pressure with open-ended questions. As the prospect shares pain, that becomes the engine that drives the urgency of the deal. Sometimes lowering the pressure with simple questions can paradoxically increase the pressure to get a deal done.

So you should be asking yourself this: outside of a proactive need for your product, why does your customer need to make a move today? Who in the business cares, and do they have the internal power to get a deal of this size done? Thinking about these kinds of questions is one of the foundational elements of a successful sale.

If you can't answer the impact and importance of a customer moving forward today, and why it is vital for their business and their personal goals, then you will be in an uphill battle. It has nothing to do with your product features, however great they may be; it has everything to do with the size of their pain. Enterprise tech sales require justification beyond simply being "proactive." What is this specific customer's motivation?

3. Avoid Too Many Choices and Narrow the Decision

When you overcomplicate pricing options, you introduce confusion where there should be simplicity. Complexity in pricing not only reduces your chances of closing a sale, you are doing a disservice to your potential customer. They need the solution you have, and yet you are making it harder for them to see clearly how to get it.

In their book *Positioning,* Al Ries and Jack Trout speak to this: "In communication, more is less. Our extravagant use of communication to solve a host of business and social problems has so jammed our channels that only a tiny fraction of all messages get through. And not necessarily the most important ones either."[8] Simple and less is almost always better.

When you go into a meeting where you will present pricing, have a specific plan in mind for what choices you will offer and in what ranges. Never offer more than three to start. (I suppose there can be exceptions to every rule, but it would be a very rare deal where there would be justification for starting off with more than three options. And for the thousands of deals I've closed, the

---

[8] Al Ries and Jack Trout, *Positioning: The Battle for Your Mind* (New York: McGraw-Hill, 2001), pg. 11.

typical is usually one or two options.) One option is appropriate when that is what is needed, as in, "This is the investment to solve all the issues you have raised."

If you choose to give three prices, start with the highest price point first, the one that you believe gives them everything they need, and some extras that will give them additional value. Outline the highlights of what this price point will give them in the simplest terms. It should be a high-level summary.

Next, give them a mid-range and again summarize. Give a one- or two-sentence reason that this is less. (Of course, sometimes the reason is that it is simply a shorter length contract.) Another example could be, "In Option A, we cover the entirety of your cloud; in Option B we just cover the Microsoft 365 components." Keep it simple and clear between options.

Lastly, give them the lowest price, and explain what it lacks compared to the other options. I hope it is obvious that you should never offer a lower price option that will not solve their main problems because that will serve no one.

It is important that at least one of the options should be within the agreed-upon price range that you confirmed with power early in the deal. And when discussing differences between options, ensure you stick to three sentences or fewer. Short, succinct, and to the point.

I'll never forget when I joined a pricing call for a rep who spent hours building six elaborate pricing options for a low-level contact. Six! By the end of the call, this non-buying IT contact asked him for three more options. The prospect never bought one of them.

Remember to keep it short, keep it simple, and only deliver the final pricing to someone who has the authority to transact on it.

4. If the Customer Asks for Something, Have Them Commit to Give Something

From your own company's perspective, you will know how much wiggle room, if any, you have on price going in. But even if you are authorized to give a little on pricing, that should not typically be where you want to start. Perhaps there are extras you can throw in that gives the customer more value but maintains the pricing presented.

If the thought of negotiating on price brings immediate stress or a tightening in your chest, I want you to think about your best friend for a moment. You would do anything for them, right? You've built years of history, and if they asked you to do them a favor (within reason, maybe even sometimes without), you would do it.

Likewise, if you really needed something, you would ask your best friend for it, right? Natural, comfortable, normal. It should be no different in being a partner with your customer. If you can truly help them solve a difficult problem, there is no reason to see it differently.

If you are solving a massive business problem for them, and now they are asking you for more favors (with money, contracts, etc.), is that something you should give on? Sometimes. But in a good and healthy partnership, you can also ask for something back—that's normal. Get comfortable with these ideas; they will serve you in your deals.

Whatever you end up giving in the negotiation, you should be considering what you may also need to get the deal closed on time at a dollar amount that meets your company's expectations.

For example: "If I am able to add the extra user licenses you want at this price, can we get a purchase order cut by Friday?"

It is perfectly right for you to negotiate in this way. If you continually give concessions without putting a commitment in play, you leave yourself open to letting things drag on well past the point that is good for anyone, including your customer. You also need to realize that oftentimes procurement will keep asking until there is a no. That is just what they do. In fact, I once had a procurement director tell me after a long negotiation at a very large Fortune 500 firm, "I was just going to keep asking for more because you hadn't told me no."

It is a good idea to build room into your deals so that you have flexibility to move with your customer's requests, but at some point, you may have to say no.

Of course, many of you reading this will sometimes get into more complicated asks from the customers that will have you relying on your deal desk or your manager before agreeing to anything. Never wing it or make stuff up about pricing on the fly, because that can backfire and destroy trust.

Do not get fancy. If you state inaccurate numbers, misquote pricing, or overcommit unapproved discounts, any of those can jeopardize entire deals. Before you join a pricing call, make sure you know where you can and can't move.

5. Cement the Decision

Many years ago, I was working with a younger rep who had done all the phenomenal work needed for a strong sale: the business pain was clear, the value aligned, the budget was identified, and power had agreed on the signoff and timing. There was one problem, though. The sales rep never guided them to make the final decision. And because there was no decision, more questions arose. So round and round the deal went, new quotes were built, mistakes were made in the process, and in the confusion of building new quotes, the sales rep mispriced the firm twice.

Procurement was furious as they assumed what was actually an honest mistake was some sort of sales trickery. It got so bad that they nearly walked. At that point, I had to step in, take over the deal, and win back trust with an option that wasn't nearly as lucrative as it should have been.

As mentioned above, we know time kills all deals. Contacts leave, get fired, die, the company goes under, is bought by a competitor, a recession hits—you name it—I have seen it happen. Indecision is often the hidden common enemy.

When we pitch our pricing and have agreement on the technical solution, you want to make the buying process as easy as possible. Visualize a funnel. Just like you move along prospects and opportunities to success or failure, within a deal, you want to narrow the funnel of decision.

Get everything that could be an obstacle out of the way of a transaction (i.e., paperwork, more questions, busy work, etc.). Limit the decision a customer has to make. Narrow focus. Once you have the quote or bundle identified, ask for the order. If a change needs to be made, get another set of eyes on it to ensure no mistakes have been made.

AGREEMENT ON PRICE?
THEN WRAP IT UP

If you came into the meeting with the goal of getting agreement on price and you get it, do not make the amateur mistake of potentially complicating or even losing the deal by going on and on with extraneous, unimportant details.

Earlier in the book, we discussed the power of using the detective or doctor persona to seek out pain and obstacles to find truths and needs that your solution can address. As your deal progresses and the opportunity has been validated, you can shift to the trial lawyer persona. This persona uses proofs, data, and logic to lead the courtroom to a decision. As in, the only reasonable verdict is to buy your solution.

This trial lawyer persona is especially useful around the time that you start presenting the final wrap-up and pricing. By clearly articulating the technical alignment, the ROI, and the problem solved with both logic and emotion, you organically lead your customers to move forward with an order by winning them over with proof after proof.

As you are near a close, verify what everyone needs to do to lock in the deal, and then wrap up the meeting. Departing in style is its own special art, and that's our next topic.

Action Steps for Chapter 7

- Price is only one factor in closing a sale. Thinking the way to get to a "yes" is by always dropping the price is a bad mindset.

- Sharing pricing near the end of a potential deal should never be a surprise. You should be validating price early and often, and with the person with the budgetary power. Also, ensure you confirm the budgetary power can sign off on a deal of your size.

- If you struggle with presenting price, reflect on whether or not your own way of handling finances and purchasing decisions is causing an issue.

- Do not add confusion by giving your prospects too many pricing options. One or two is usually best; three is the maximum.

- Prepare for pricing calls with procurement by knowing your red lines and where you can give. Find a way to narrow down the funnel and clear obstacles to get to a yes.

- When it is time to close the deal, switch to the persona of a trial lawyer, making a final summation by clear logic. Then get an agreement and get out!

CHAPTER 8

DEPARTING IN STYLE

*"All the world's a stage, and all
the men and women merely players;
they have their exits and
their entrances..."*

—WILLIAM SHAKESPEARE

ONE DAY IN 2006, I WAS out horseback riding with friends a couple of hours outside New York City, and I got a call from my agent about auditioning for a role on *The Sopranos*. Could I get to the HBO offices in Manhattan tomorrow?

Uh, yeah. I think I might be able to carve out some time for that.

At the time, *The Sopranos* was probably the most prestigious television series on the air and was having a huge impact on the culture. The part on offer was a small role and not recurring, but still

—*The Sopranos*! That was a show that almost any actor would jump at the chance to be associated with.

Not to mention, if I could land it, that would make for a "great piece of tape," as actors like to say. (Tape = a video of your highlights as an actor to use to get more work. It's kind of the equivalent of having a great personal case study in sales.)

As my agent told me about it, things just kept sounding better and better. He said that they had to book this fast, meaning only a handful of actors would be considered. And there wouldn't be any "callbacks," an industry term where you have to come back for multiple auditions before you get the part or don't.

"They will probably be booking this right from the meeting," he said.

That is music to an actor's ears. No agonizing waits and a good chance of securing the role on the spot.

I had less than a day to prepare, but that didn't matter much in this case. Television shows like *The Sopranos* keep a tight rein on scripts because they do not want a bunch of them floating around. If they didn't keep it highly controlled, no doubt spoilers for upcoming shows would end up online.

But not having a script did not worry me too much; by then, I had a lot of professional experience under my belt, and I figured if they were looking to get this role booked quickly, I had an inside track and just needed to do what I was trained to do.

The next day there, I was walking the halls of HBO, with all the posters of their legendary shows on display. I'm getting more and more pumped up with every step.

I ended up in the room with the casting director and one other person. A lot of times, these "cold read" auditions are very basic, with very little interaction. You come in and do your performance, and you leave. But this was different. We started off with some friendly, engaging conversation. I feel even better, and I'm thinking, "This is so great. We're hitting it off."

Next, the casting director tells me, "We're booking today. We shoot tomorrow, and it will probably be three days on set." She checks to make sure I could do that. I feel even closer to grabbing this part. Just that month, I had booked two commercials and a print campaign with casting directors that had more or less used the same words and process for confirming availability. I'm thinking, "This is my role. Let's go!"

Next, it's time to read the script, and I dive in. When I finish, the casting director is looking at me funny.

I asked if something was wrong. Did she need me to re-do it? Should I do something differently?

The word "on" was in the script, and she asked me to say the word again. I said it again.

"I don't think this is going to work," she said. "Your pronunciation of that word is not right for what we need."

Apparently, my mid-Atlantic US way of saying "on" would not be right for this character. I start to feel this part slip from my grasp, but at the same time, I'm an actor. I can certainly get into the voice of another character. "I can say 'on' how you need it done in the role."

"I'm sorry, we just can't risk it," the casting director told me. As much as it hurt, I could see it from her point of view. As I noted in Chapter 5, these shows are incredibly expensive to make, and every minute of every scene is precious from a budget standpoint. If I said "on" wrong in the moment, and they had to do a re-take or two because of it, that could cost thousands and thousands of dollars.

I still believed I would have been able to say it in character, but at that point, there was nothing to do but accept the verdict and try to leave the room with as much grace as possible, despite the crushing disappointment.

As I rise up out of the chair, I don't stand up in the regular way. Because I had just been horse riding the day before, I swung my leg over unnaturally, almost as if I was dismounting the chair. It must have been a combination of horse riding soreness and muscle memory from the day before. Whatever the reason, I found it amusing.

I saw an opportunity for a little self-deprecating humor, figuring I would show them I could handle rejection with dignity and good wit.

"Did you guys just see that?" I said with a little chuckle. "I just got off that chair like I was climbing off a horse. What am I doing?"

The casting director and the other person in the room stared back at me stone-faced. Apparently, the answer was, "No, they didn't see that, and they had no idea what I might be doing." From their perspective, they still didn't have a much-needed role filled, and I was now eating up precious time. They weren't going to throw me even so much as a smile for my efforts to lighten things up. I understood—they had work to do. Okay, it was now official. This hadn't gone well.

But my dream-turned-to-nightmare audition wasn't quite over yet. For the final act, I turned to leave, reaching for the nearest door, the one I thought I came in. I opened it, and it was a closet. I sheepishly closed it, put on my best "play-it-off" smile, and found the right door.

Talk about departing in style. As the door closed behind me, I didn't know whether to laugh or cry.

Let's review. I went into this audition super excited to have an inside track on a role on one of the most prestigious television series of all time that would have me on set the very next day, likely with the legend James Gandolfini. A few minutes later, I left, rejected based on my pronunciation of a two-letter word. An attempt at humor fell completely flat. And then I tried to exit through a closet.

Honestly, I am not sure I could have done anything about what happened in that room that particular day. Everything seemed to have hinged on the tiny pronunciation issue, something I couldn't have known or prepared for going in. Sometimes you just have a lousy day, and everything that can go wrong does go wrong.

Looking back, though, I do wonder whether the fact that I was so excited about this role, and that I could almost feel it in my grasp, led me to lose a little focus.

Either way, days like this are why we lay a foundation of good physical, mental, and emotional health. We can bounce back from those Murphy's Law days because we have a strong, healthy base. And we always focus on controlling what we can control, and not on those things we can't.

The concept of controlling what we can control is crucial in both the life of an actor and in the art of sales meetings. Too often, we chalk things up that go wrong to bad luck when, in fact, we mishandled the situation. And sometimes, we don't even realize we have made a mistake. That's a problem.

A MISTAKE I SEE ALL TOO FREQUENTLY

How you end the meeting—whether you "depart in style" or not—will make a big difference in how your potential customer evaluates the overall meeting. Maya Angelou said, "I've learned that people will forget what you said, people will forget what you did, but people will never forget how you made them feel."

I believe that to be true, and how you make people feel has a lot to do with the final impression you leave them. I would go so far as to say that the ability to depart in style is one of the key distinguishing markers between reps who come across as disorganized greenhorns versus reps who reveal themselves to be meeting masters.

Okay, but how do you do it? What practical steps can you take to always "depart in style?" The first rule is to make sure you budget adequate time at the end of a meeting for a proper wrap-up.

When you fail to do this, it almost always results in a chaotic end to the meeting, where next steps are not clearly agreed to and outlined. Do you know those movies where there is a whole bunch of chaotic action, and you are wondering how everything can wrap up all the storylines in time? Then the ending does come, and you discover the filmmaker slapped on something in the last five minutes that does not make a lot of sense, and then just basically says, "The End." You are left with a feeling of confusion, and you have lost some trust and respect for the filmmaker.

This is exactly what your prospective customers will think and feel about a meeting that ends abruptly. Instead of adequate time to discuss whether the meeting goal has been met and map out clear next steps, you are leaving everyone involved with an uneasy feeling of confusion and uncertainty.

So let me give you an exceptionally clear and practical rule: Always set aside at least fifteen minutes to wrap up the meeting. (Sometimes you can get away with ten minutes, but it's better to have a little more than you need than too little.) If you are taking notes or highlighting passages in this book, let me repeat this one more time, so you are sure to mark it: Always set aside at least fifteen minutes to wrap up a meeting!

When you fail to watch the clock and do not leave adequate time, you leave yourself with three choices, all of them less than ideal:

- Make an attempt to impose on the customer by going over the meeting time. The customer may not even be able to do this, but even if they agree, it makes you look like someone who doesn't respect their time sufficiently.

- Rush through crucial wrap-up steps at lightning speed, which will lead to important things being missed and the customer having an impression of you as scattered.
- You can end the meeting without clearly outlined next steps, and without a next meeting set. If you do this, your only option is to try to make up for this in follow-up emails, which may fail. You then have to go back to the hamster wheel of chasing folks down just to get back on a calendar. With this failed approach of no clear next steps or responsibilities, you have likely lost momentum with this customer, and getting things back on track may be very difficult.

All this can be avoided by simply having the discipline to begin wrap-up with plenty of time left. If your sales engineer is talking, but it is time for wrap-up, you need to be the quarterback. Take back control during the final fifteen minutes. Most inexperienced reps figure about five minutes or less should work, but that will rarely be enough time. As stated above, fifteen minutes is a good guide for most situations, but of course, you may need to allow for more time in some circumstances.

There is another consideration for the pace of the meeting that you need to be alert to. There will be times when a key source of power for the deal will be scheduled to leave before the meeting ends. When you know that, it is essential that you plan for their scheduled departure time by covering the most important things before they leave.

And instead of waiting until the end of the meeting to define and confirm clear next steps, do that before the "power" leaves the meeting. If you don't, you potentially could lose your only chance at having critical budget and timing questions answered, or even miss the opportunity to confirm the deal itself. It is important to adjust for these kinds of differing circumstances as you time out your meeting.

WHAT TO ACCOMPLISH
DURING WRAP UP

Planning out the time is an important first step, but then you need to know what specifically to cover in the wrap-up.

Specific endings will depend on the context of each meeting. A very common one is where you accomplished some of what you needed to, but there is more that needs to be done.

In cases like this, it is best to say something along the lines of, "I see we have roughly fifteen minutes today. We have accomplished [X and Y] today, but it does not look like we will have time to get [Z] achieved today. Can we take a minute to set the next time to meet?"

Then get down to the nitty-gritty of getting on to everyone's calendar right then and there if at all possible. Set responsibilities and action items for yourself and for the various players on your prospect's side. If you do not, it is going to be super challenging to organize a time later when all the key players are available.

Once you have the next meeting time set, circle back and summarize the goals that you did accomplish in an email. When possible, recap what certain people called out and use their name when summarizing.

"Jim talked about [potential issue] and if it was possible to get around it, and we agreed that we could avoid this by [solution]."

(As a side note here, make good, quick notes to yourself during this part of the meeting especially. It will help when you follow up, which we will cover extensively in the next chapter.)

Once you have summarized the goals you have met, clearly define the next step. In the example above, you did that by setting the next meeting, so you would just repeat the date and the goal for the next meeting.

Other times the next step will have multiple parts. Maybe it will involve the steps needed to cut a purchase order. Maybe it will be gathering needed technical detail to begin a trial phase. Whatever it is, be crystal clear on what the steps are and who is responsible for each.

Once all that is set, show sincere gratitude for their time—then get the heck out of Dodge! Let me explain what I mean by each of these statements.

Sincere Gratitude

Too often, sales reps have this image in their heads that forced small talk at the end of the meeting is a requirement. This is to think of sales as about fakery, where you must check off the box marked, "Ask them about their kids."

Customers will sense the awkwardness and recognize it for what it is. If you have had time to establish a relationship with some or all of the participants, then asking them sincere questions about their kids, their summer, a common interest, or whatever else is perfectly fine, as long as it comes from a place of sincerity.

But if you don't have that kind of relationship yet, do not force it.

One thing you can always do at the end of a meeting is show sincere gratitude. And I hope it is sincere because remember you are there to live out your mission to solve problems and relieve pain for them. Assuming you are following the advice in this book, you are also closing a lot of sales and are well compensated for it. If you are not grateful for all those things, I cannot help you.

When I say sincere gratitude, of course, I don't mean you have to fall all over yourself with fawning thank yous and over-the-top gestures. A direct thank you for their time while making eye contact around the room is plenty. In many cases, you will also want to walk out with your reseller partner who set up the meeting or with your "champion" at the company and give them an individual thank you.

Treats

For some meetings, it will be appropriate to bring treats (or have them delivered). Sometimes it will be something catered for during the meeting, but other times it will be something left behind for the customer to enjoy. A few things to consider:

- Leaving behind something of high-quality will have your company name being talked about after you leave. ("Who brought these amazing cookies?") Because of this, you are going to want to make sure you bring them something of memorable quality and not be remembered for the wrong reason.

- Along these same lines, if you are bringing in lunch for them at the end of a late morning meeting, don't pick up the sandwiches on the way and put them out an hour or so later, soggy and unappealing. Get them delivered by a good caterer right near the end of the meeting.

- It does not always have to be food. Swag and other small items can be a fun leave behind. The important thing is to be thoughtful about what you are bringing and to give it to them quickly and unobtrusively. Keep in mind that many folks are concerned with swag that is environmentally wasteful these days. Be cognizant of what your customers desire.

- In certain situations, treats will be inappropriate and even illegal. If your potential customer is the government or associated with a government contractor, you will want to avoid any rule-breaking or anything that could put someone in a bad spot.

Now—Get the Heck Out!

Exits for an actor are often an opportunity for some of the richest and most emotional moments in the craft of performance. From a comedic pratfall on the way out a door to a storming off stage, these moments are a chance to end the scene or story with a bang or a cathartic moment. What these memorable exits typically have in common is that at their peak, they are powerfully condensed in a moment that packs a wallop.

This can actually be seen best when it is intentionally done poorly. Consider a vivid death scene. Done right, it is one of the most impactful moments an actor can portray. But when drawn out to absurd lengths, it makes us laugh instead. Think *Tropic Thunder*, *Zoolander*, *The Naked Gun*, or *Austin Powers*—they all played ridiculously drawn-out death scenes for laughs.

Think about this the next time you are tempted to keep going and going because you are too nervous to wrap it up. Stretching out endings can become absurd, although when you do it, it won't be played for laughs. It will just damage your chances to earn the sale. You have probably heard the show business expression, "Always leave them wanting more," and that is a good mindset to have.

Of course, by this, I don't mean anything like leaving them confused or unclear on next steps. This is more about being a confident professional who comes in, solves problems, and then lets the customer get back to their day. Do not come across as needy or as a person who is unsure of how to wrap it up.

Examples

You have a phone meeting early in the process where a person agrees to set up an in-person meeting with someone with power. Get the details settled, and then get off the phone. There's no need to stay for chit-chatting.

Someone agrees to the pricing structure you outlined. Your response should be, "That's great; I will get you the actionable quote within an hour." And then quickly wrap things up and leave the room.

Obviously, do not take this too literally to the point of abruptness. But I have seen reps meet the goal for the meeting and then mess up the deal by going on and on and saying irrelevant stuff or, in some cases, inappropriate stuff that damages their chance of a sale. You are on a mission to help your customers. Do it, and then don't waste their time.

Your underlying message to your clients should be: "I honor your time. I value my own time. I'm efficient, confident, and professional. Because of all this, you know that I do what I say, and so you can trust me when I say we can solve this problem." When you efficiently close out meetings and then are on your way, these are the messages you send.

One Final Warning

Years ago, I remember witnessing an embarrassing scene at the end of a meeting that can serve as a warning about getting too comfortable with your customer. I was leaving a meeting set up by a reseller. The reseller and one of the people from the customer company had an established relationship, and so they felt extremely comfortable joking around with each other.

The problem was that as they left the meeting, they apparently forgot they were not out on the town or going to a ballgame together. They were still in a corporate environment. They were talking extremely loudly, joking about things that weren't office appropriate, and spiking their talk with salty language.

I was embarrassed enough to see this as heads in the office kept turning toward this spectacle. But then, when someone from another division in the company had to come down the hall and tell them they were disturbing the whole office, that made it truly awful to witness.

This is the kind of behavior that can wreck deals and earn you a reputation you do not want. Show respect for where you are, and be appropriate to the situation. It is a wonderful thing to have a fantastic, comfortable relationship with business colleagues and customers, but do not get so comfortable you forget where you are.

YOU JUST SEPARATED YOURSELF FROM ABOUT 90 PERCENT OF THE REPS OUT THERE

As we wrap up this chapter, I'm compelled to highlight just how crucial the concept of "Departing in Style" is to mastering meetings. The great thing is that none of what you learned in this chapter is a challenging skill that needs practice over and over to master it. These are all "planning ahead" actions that anyone can do. To summarize, always do the following:

- Leave PLENTY of time for wrap-up—typically at least fifteen minutes.
- Confirm that the goal for the meeting was met and provide a concise recap.
- Make sure you know what the key decision-maker (the Power) needs to see before they leave the meeting. Always keep in mind different powers will be looking for different things. What information the budget power needs will likely be different from what the technical power needs to know, etc.
- Define the clear next step and who owns what actions, and then document it in an email.
- Show sincere gratitude and then get the heck out!

Do those things and people will recognize you as a person who adds value and solves problems, and you'll leave everyone feeling like their time was well spent.

Of course, departing in style is not the end of it. You need to follow-up, often persistently. There's an art to that, too, which is the subject of the next chapter.

Action Steps for Chapter 8

- Rule number one is to leave yourself plenty of time for wrap-up. Many inexperienced reps run out of time and mess up the ending. Take charge and begin wrapping up fifteen minutes before the scheduled end of the meeting.

- Do not go on too long at the end. Be concise and efficient and get everyone focused on next steps.

- Ensure everyone is on the same page on the next steps and the driving call to action. Who needs to achieve what this week so we all hit the project deadline? Understanding the impact of the project's success to your customer's bottom line is what will make these actions a priority.

- If leaving behind treats or providing food/refreshments for the meeting, be sure to confirm that it is all set-up so there are no embarrassing snags.

- Be conscious of how you are leaving the office after a meeting. Never be loud or make a spectacle of yourself.

CHAPTER 9

FOLLOWING UP

"Ever tried. Ever failed.
No matter. Try again.
Fail again. Fail better."

—SAMUEL BECKETT

THE MOTIVATION FOR ACTORS TO PUSH through the daily tedium and stress of following up to get parts they want is naturally strong. It is a little like prospecting, except imagine doing it for no money. Or having audition after audition, but with a much higher rate of failure than sales meetings. That is the actor's dilemma. The magic of being on the stage or screen and the love of the craft inspires you to keep going, but success can be more elusive.

One of my favorite audition stories was when I had a chance for the lead in a network television show. It was early in my career, I was green and did not even have an agent yet. I was fortunate to even have a shot because a generous agent who had seen me perform in an off-off Broadway play decided to give me a shot and submitted me for the role.

I recognized it for the opportunity it was and prepared for it like it was my last chance at a gig ever. I hired coaches, reworked scenes again and again, and worked late into the night to strengthen my performance.

On top of all that, the audition was at a studio that was ninety minutes away, a trip I had to make five times in total. From what I was told for this role, they started the search globally with hundreds of professional actors and after multiple rounds of auditions, it came down to me and one other guy.

In the end, I did not get it. As disappointing as that was, it did not go to waste. For one thing, it gave me some confidence because my gut review of my performance was that I worked up near the very top of the range of my skills at the time. As they say in sports, I left it all on the field.

It also had more tangible benefits. Numerous other opportunities grew directly from that audition. In both acting and sales, I have found that showing up as a professional and being persistent in both effort and follow-up always has a positive payoff of some kind. And when you consistently show up as a professional, casting directors talk to each other (just like your prospects—CISOs, CIOs, and CFOs—do).

While there are differences between the amount of success you can expect from good follow-up in sales versus acting, there is also some overlap. If you want to score a principal role on a major network show, not only will you have multiple callbacks, you can expect to need sign-offs from a network executive, the writer, the producer, the casting director, and potentially also the director and star of the show. Miss with any of them, and you won't get the job.

To close a big tech deal, you may need the go-ahead from the CISO, the General Counsel, the Director of Infrastructure, the Director of Privacy, CFO, CIO, and CEO and potentially others. Miss with any of them, and you will not get the sale.

Here's where the difference in success comes in, though, and why salespeople should count their blessings. In my experience, for most sales deals you have much more control in whether you close it than an actor ever does over his role.

That is not to say that you have total control, of course. But if you are getting to power quickly, verifying there is a problem you can help them solve, and validating on price early and often, you will win a lot of deals. It just requires staying on top of things and following up doggedly.

All this reminds me of a common saying in sales: the fortune is in the follow-up. That might sound like a cliché, but in my experience it also happens to be true. Reps that are the best at consistent and skilled follow up are the ones who blow past their quota and rack up huge commissions, year after year. They do this while also fulfilling their client's project needs.

One crucial component of follow-up is very simple: *actually do it*. Actors are generally passionate about their craft, and so the motivation for the grind is often built-in. It also comes out of necessity; if you don't book the role, you don't eat.

In sales, we should be as passionate about our work, but I witness many times where we allow distractions or lesser priorities to keep us from our most important tasks (which are prospecting, getting meetings, executing in meetings, and follow-up). Are you as motivated as a hungry actor is in your follow-up?

You should be because as a salesperson, you have a big advantage over the actor. Follow-up in acting only gives you a shot at success—a kind of success where the financial rewards tend to be inconsistent.

In sales, if you do follow-up consistently, you WILL succeed. Not in every single instance, of course, but enough times to make it very financially rewarding. Also, the bulk of senior tech sellers are making a far higher base pay than most folks outside of our industry could ever dream of. Are you honoring the opportunity before you?

As I have tried to get across in several different ways in this book, all it takes is a motivation and dedication to your craft that matches the intensity that most actors bring to learning their craft. In sales, you will succeed if you put in the passion and hard work.

You might be saying, "Yes, I'm in! I do want to pour myself into my craft. But what specific actions should I be taking to follow up in the most effective way possible?"

That's the exact right question, and I'll share some best practices in just a moment. First, though, a small detour to remind you that sometimes follow-up is a bad idea.

WHEN NOT TO FOLLOW UP

Having a "no-quit" philosophy is mega-valuable in sales. For example, being able to push through cold call after cold call and other prospecting methods is a huge factor in sales success. Or having the fortitude to practice a difficult meeting skill until you master it is another place where a "never say die" attitude comes in handy.

There are times, though, when gritting your teeth and trying to continue to push through barriers is a bad idea. This can definitely be true when it comes to following up with a prospect that turns out not to be a good fit.

If you are feeling too eager for the sale, that's when you will override signs of a mismatch and put on your "happy sales ears" to convince yourself that it can still work, even when you are getting clear indications that this will go nowhere.

Remember that one of the reasons you are constantly validating leads, getting to power as quickly as possible, and making sure you have alignment on price is to also know when to *disqualify* a prospect.

Every minute you spend on a company that is not truly a match for your products and services is a minute you could have spent finding and nurturing a company that is a match. You are doing the prospective company a favor, too, by not wasting their time on a solution that won't solve their problem or is outside their budget. You also will avoid using up people and resources in your own company by involving them in meetings and forecasting sales that will not bear any fruit.

In short, there's no heroism in continuing to follow up with a company that is not a good fit. It actually creates a negative value.

If you find yourself often trying to still sell and continually follow up when there is not a fit, you need to dig deeper and ask yourself why that is happening. It is almost always because you do not have a strong pipeline of prospects, and so you feel pressure to turn every meeting into an eventual sale.

And quality prospecting is where this journey begins. Strong prospecting means you don't have to try and keep after deals that either won't or shouldn't happen. I recall a story from my early days where a new SDR, Benny, came along like a house of fire. Benny began by breaking records by doubling the leader on the meeting board—he was averaging sixty meetings a quarter!

The top execs were eating it up. "Look at that, Benny won the two hundred dollar spiff for most meetings booked." But it turned out he was showboating and smirking his way through, and in the end, about 10 percent of his meetings showed, and most of those were absolute garbage.

Still, somehow Benny was later promoted to a field role but quickly fizzled out because he never broke the poor habit of putting style over substance. He never trusted himself and his work. His attention was on getting "meetings" and looking good and the quick fix, not on what it took to book a deal.

Meetings don't matter. Good and validated meetings matter, and quantity alone never wins. We need quantity and quality to succeed. This is why a consistent, quality pipeline is so important for your confidence in meetings. Imagine how much you separate yourself from the standard image of the desperate salesperson willing to try anything to close the sale.

Distinguish yourself by saying, "From what I am hearing, it is sounding like we are not a good match because [whatever the reason—budget, etc.] That's fine; it was good that we met to explore this and figure that out. If this eventually becomes a priority for you, I'd be happy to jump on a call." And then you exit gracefully, without trying to push something on them. When you have strong prospecting habits you have plenty of opportunities if a particular one does not pan out, which then allows you to demonstrate this kind of confidence in your meetings.

So there will be times when it is time not to follow-up. But of course, the majority of times, once you land a meeting, you will find a good fit, and that's when excellent follow-up will be essential to your getting deals across the finish line.

But what specifically should you do?

PRACTICAL STEPS
FOR GREAT FOLLOW-UP

Let me say right from the start that different kinds of deals, meetings, and sales processes will necessitate adjustments to how you follow up. What follows is not intended to be a one-size-fits-all, step-by-step way to follow up. Still, the principles here and the examples will serve you well if you take them seriously.

The Recap Email

There is one kind of follow-up that you should do after every single meeting with a partner or customer. It is simple and takes relatively little time, but yet so many reps fail to do it consistently, and sometimes not at all. I'm referring to a recap email.

The email recap has value out of proportion to the time it takes to send it. For one thing, it marks you out as a conscientious professional. More importantly, every person in the meeting has a busy schedule. In two or three days, most people will remember the meeting at a high-level but will not be able to recall every key detail. Your email serves as a record of the highlights for anyone to review at any point (including yourself).

Most important of all, it outlines the key next step (or next steps) and who is responsible for what before the next meeting. Both you and your customer may have different action items to take responsibility for, and the email recap is a perfect way to outline this. Remember, having a clear next step/goal is incredibly important to keeping on track to get a sale across the finish line.

What should you rely on to write a good email recap? Don't say "memory."

Over the years, I have observed that the top sales reps at any company are amazing note- takers. I'm actually baffled by the high number of reps I've seen in my career who sit in a meeting and don't take a single note. Those reps that claim to "keep it all in my head" never seem to achieve anything remotely close in bonuses as the great note-takers do.

Note-taking in meetings is something you should work hard to get better at, but also remember not to bury your head in your laptop or consistently lose eye contact with your meeting participants. I'd highly recommend bringing a pen and your favorite journal. And spend some time practicing being able to take notes while keeping your eyes and head up on what's going on in the room.

You want good, specific notes on the main topics discussed, what obstacles remain, and who is responsible for next actions. Your notes should also record important individual comments and objections, unique pains and timelines, who cares about what, and any questions you couldn't fully answer in the moment.

Take all your great notes and create a concise summary of the meeting, pulling out the key details. If you overload it with extraneous information, people will take one glance at it and decide to read it later. And later may not happen.

Three things to include in all your recap emails:

- What was accomplished today?
- What are the specific next steps, and who is responsible for each of them? There may be responsibilities on your side and on your prospect's side. Address them by specific people (color coding this in an email may help bring it to attention).
- When the next meeting is scheduled (or provide a link to your calendar to get it scheduled).

Get the recap email out as soon as possible, and certainly by the end of the business day on which the meeting occurred. Schedule the recap on your calendar for later in the day if you face one of those days with back-to-back meetings. Although it is easy to forget, a professional does not let this slip.

Following Up on Your Follow Up

People often forget to confirm meeting invites. It is also not at all uncommon for your recap email to quickly slide down your customer's inbox, and they fail to get you the key information they promised or fail to take the action needed to meet the next goal.

These types of issues are all part of the process. Accept that following up on your original follow-up will be necessary quite often; you should just expect it. Don't complain about it; just get it done. However, don't just be the annoying person that sends whiny reminders. Remember that any communication is a chance to add value.

Here's an example:

Hi John,

In our last meeting, you mentioned that identifying the critical and sensitive data on your servers by June 15 is an absolute necessity to meet your audit requirements. Per our discussion, it will take a week to do the scanning.

It's now May 30, and I just want to make sure that we are tracking for that end date. If you can get me the sign-off for the install by tomorrow June 1, you will still be able to meet your critical deadline. Can you confirm with your team that we are good for the install tomorrow?

This is the kind of follow-up email you can send to get a stalled situation back on track, and you can only be this specific if you have done a great job of uncovering the problems and the pain behind it. The value the customer gets from this email is both a reminder of what is at stake and a solution with a specific timeline. This is the kind of email that gets a response when deadlines start to slip, and you are not getting responses fast enough.

A good point here is if you don't get a response after multiple tries, then something is up. It could be personnel changes, budget changes, or maybe your contact is in the middle of a serious personal matter. Regardless, the spidey senses should go up, because not only is the customer not responding, they aren't responding to their own deadlines and needs.

Either something was missed in the original meeting about understanding priorities or the project is in serious jeopardy (or both). Stay on top of your communication when this happens to get a handle on the true status of the deal.

Leveraging Your Follow Up
to "Climb the Ladder" to Power

You have to understand that the quality of your follow-up from meetings can and should be much better than in prospecting follow-ups. When you are prospecting, you only know what you can glean and guess from your research. Once you start meeting with a company, you should start to leverage the information and contacts you get in each meeting to "climb the ladder."

If you can get to power right away with no previous meetings, that's what you should do. But often your first contact will be with middle management. There you explore the pain, the problem, and the budget as best you can. If things seem to be in alignment, you want to then get a meeting with power to validate that your solution is an important company priority.

If a mid-level person has not followed up and scheduled a meeting with a decision maker, your next effort could look something like this:

Hi Lauren,

The last time we met, you said you thought our solution could help your VP Jane meet her goals for the upcoming project.

There were four things we said we should discuss with Jane:

[BULLET LIST OF THOSE 4 THINGS]

I know you said solving this problem was a high priority for your leadership team and that it is something that needs to be accomplished within three months before your fiscal year ends.

Is there a time we can find to get on Jane's calendar together? Here is a link to my calendar where you can book an open spot with me.

Do you notice how specific you can be with following up with potential customers once you are in a cycle of meetings with them?

It is more detailed than you can ever be in following up with prospects.

And remember that here again, you are adding value for your customer with this kind of follow-up. By outlining exactly what can be accomplished, when it can be accomplished, and why it is important to accomplish it, you are delivering value. In the example above, you have teed things up nicely for Lauren to follow through and set the meeting with Jane and make herself look good in the process.

One other little detail to notice here. The email references a link to a calendar scheduling app that allows for easy scheduling. Do yourself a favor and use this kind of calendar tool. It is more preferred than sending out suggested times to multiple people, which can lead to cumbersome and time-wasting back and forth.

AVOID DEAL STOPPERS

Watch Out for Deal Derailers

One thing to be sensitive to is people who can derail a deal. This can come from a place not of true opposition, but where a person does not have a good grasp of the benefits of the solution you can provide. It may also come from a person who wants the budget for a different solution or project altogether.

One of the most common ways this comes about is when a key person missed an important meeting. They only hear snippets of what is going on, but just enough for them to object or not fully understand the value. If they are copied on your recap email, they may begin to fire off a lot of questions and concerns.

My suggestion is to invite this person to a one-on-one meeting to bring them up to speed. This meeting can serve three purposes. For one, you can get a sense of the person—who they are, what they care about, how you can make them successful in their role, and what they may be missing about your solution. Two, you can personalize the meeting to the specific concerns and objections they may be raising. And three, sometimes this can turn a person from a skeptic to an ally because of the one-on-one connection that is established in the meeting.

It is this kind of detailed work and personalized follow-up that can make or break an enterprise deal, or stop it from going to a competitor. Don't skimp on making efforts like this.

Getting the Tech Right

Many of you reading this book will have a sales process that involves doing a trial before a final purchase order is cut.

This is where you want to bring your "quarterback" skills into play and make sure you are coordinating and following up with your team, so nothing falls through the cracks. It is especially important that you stay in lock step with your sales engineer.

For example, if you just sent a recap email that shares trial install dates, it is crucial that your sales engineer deliver the technical details of server needs and or API configurations ASAP. There is nothing worse than getting a commitment to move forward and then lacking the technical information that allows the next step to be executed. Follow up quickly with any member of your team before it becomes a major issue.

You have now been taken through everything you need to master the art of sales meetings. But this is a journey that is never done, and the final chapter is all about how to go on a journey of never-ending improvement.

Action Steps for Chapter 9

- The old sales proverb that "The fortune is in the follow-up" is true. You can't be successful without high-quality, consistent follow-up.

- Remember that having a "no quit" mindset is not the same as continuing to chase a prospect who should be disqualified (for lack of a budget or lack of urgency or for having a problem that is not a match for your solution). It is no virtue to keep following up with prospects where the chance of a sale is extremely marginal.

- Always do a recap email after each meeting. Summarize what was accomplished, detail who is responsible for each action item before the next meeting, and remind/confirm the next meeting time.

- After each meeting, consider whether you are making progress. Are you leveraging your prior meeting to get the next one, each time moving up the ladder of power?

- Great follow-up is always about having a clear next step for your team and your prospect's team.

- Identify the key call to action for this week for your meetings and deals that will move the needle. Own or delegate the action to ensure you stay on track for success.

- Remember that you are the quarterback. Keep your team coordinated and on the same page throughout each meeting and throughout the entire sales cycle.

CHAPTER 10

DIRECTOR'S NOTES

"I think a good director is
a good listener."

—DENIS VILLENEUVE

THERE I WAS, ALL OF SIXTEEN years old, and on a movie set watching Tom Cruise and Steven Spielberg huddling between scenes for the movie *The Minority Report*.

Watching them was, of course, thrilling to my teenage self because it was two of the most famous guys in the world. But beyond the surface level, watching them in that moment impressed a deeper lesson on me, and it is one directly relevant to becoming great at conducting sales meetings.

But first things first. Let me circle back and tell you how this came about.

Back then, I had a summer job building decks. I liked having some teenage spending money and that I could work on my tan on the job. These were my big teenage concerns that summer, and acting was the furthest thing from my mind at that point.

So I was floored when I came home from work one day, and my sisters surrounded me, excitedly shouting, "You're going to be in a movie!"

To which I gave the only sane response: "What are you talking about?"

Without me knowing it, they had submitted my picture and resume to be an "extra" in the movie, *The Minority Report*. By my resume, they meant some child acting I had done in commercials, films, and theater. It wasn't extensive, and I had not done any kind of performing for at least eight years, nor had I taken any acting classes since way back then.

The news that I was going to be on set for the filming of a Spielberg–Cruise movie was a shocker, to say the least, but I certainly was not going to turn down the chance. Especially at sixteen, the perks of being an extra on a big-budget movie are great.

You typically get paid a couple of hundred bucks for longer days, there can be some great catered meals, and you get to experience the set with all its energy and action. The scene was set in the heart of Washington, DC, in what was then the brand new Ronald Reagan building.

This was nearly two decades ago, and many of the details from my days on set have faded. But I do remember two things quite distinctly. One was that I was lined up to fulfill my role as an extra in a scene directly behind Tom Cruise. I was going to be in this thing! But then I got moved for being too tall. Even at sixteen, I was over six feet tall, and Cruise was quite a bit shorter. That is not a contrast that is going to be allowed with the lead actor in a movie.

A bit disappointing, but those are the breaks. (And if you are wondering if I am in the movie—I'm really not sure. There's one scene where I think if you look in the far, top left corner and you don't blink, it might be me.)

The other thing I remember well is when Cruise initially walked onto the set. There was the commotion you might expect when a movie superstar walks on set, particularly in an outside setting like that with a lot of people around.

But it is what happened next that really caught my attention. Cruise and Spielberg got right to work shooting the scene. But then they would stop, and they would come together and be intensely talking about what they were doing. Of course, I was not privy to exactly what they were saying. But you could tell from body language and gestures that they were all business, and hyper-focused on analyzing details.

It made an instant impression on me. Suddenly what I was seeing had nothing to do with fame and everything to do with two people who were exceptionally serious about their craft. Part of my surprise probably came from the fact that I was still a teenager.

But I still think it is very easy for all of us to imagine people at the top of their professions as these gifted talents to whom everything comes naturally. We think, "It's Spielberg. He is so skilled and experienced he just automatically knows exactly what he wants and pronounces it."

Or, "He's Cruise. He just shows up, looks good, and does his thing." Of course, they both have crazy amounts of talent, and maybe a touch of genius in their respective areas of expertise.

However, watching them in that moment, the seeds of a lesson were planted in me. Over time, it is a lesson that has been confirmed for me again and again in both my acting and sales careers.

The lesson: it doesn't matter who you are or how talented you may be; to do something great takes a commitment to hard work, and that includes constantly questioning and reviewing what you are doing to get better each day. It also means being open to learning from others, be they teachers, coaches, or colleagues.

As the saying goes, hard work beats talent when talent doesn't work hard. One of my favorite writers on this subject is Steven Pressfield, author of *Gates of Fire*, *The Legend of Bagger Vance*, and more.

In his book *The War of Art*, Pressfield delivers a number of thought-provoking insights on attacking the day as a professional. He calls overcoming obstacles to productivity battling "Resistance."

In one chapter, he states:

A Professional does not hesitate to ask for help. Tiger Woods is the greatest golfer in the world. Yet he has a teacher... It would never occur to him, as it would to an amateur, that he knows everything or can figure everything out on his own. On the contrary, he seeks out the most knowledgeable teacher and listens with both ears. The student of the game knows that the levels of revelation that can unfold in golf, as in art, are inexhaustible.[9]

Those sales reps who think that they will get by on talent or looks or fast talk or any other sales cliché are the ones who do not make it or always remain mediocre. The ones who are mega-successful are like Spielberg and Cruise. They know that true craftsmen get right down to work, and they constantly analyze their performance to get better.

Progress happens faster when you proactively seek constructive feedback in all its forms. What are some of the ways to get great feedback, and what do you do with it when you get it? That's the subject of the rest of this chapter.

TAKE PRIDE IN WHAT YOU DO

Let's first remind ourselves of one of the fundamental mindsets you need to keep improving: if you want to become great at the art of the sales meeting, treat it like an art. By that, I mean take pride in what you do and respect that it is something worth becoming exceptional for its own sake.

Acting is known as an art, and it is an extremely competitive field. This means that most actors realize they have to push themselves

---

[9] Steven Pressfield, *The War of Art: Break Through the Blocks and Win Your Inner Creative Battles* (New York: Black Irish Entertainment LLC, 2002), pg. 85.

to have any chance to excel. The expectation to be motivated and detailed about craft comes with the territory.

Unfortunately, and although paid significantly more than most workers in the country just in their base pay alone, many tech salespeople do not recognize that the art of meetings is also a craft and that to get great at it requires a similar dedication and commitment. But this sad fact is also an opportunity for you to stand out in a big way. You can bypass 90 percent of your fellow tech salespeople if you do the work and embrace the commitment to become a master of your craft.

Here's another way to say it: it is time for you to go on a quest.

THE RELENTLESS QUEST

You will never reach your full potential as a salesperson, especially in meetings, without going on a relentless quest to get better. You should, of course, analyze your performance on a macro level, but to truly become excellent, you need to also dig down to the granular level.

Where is the best place to start getting granular? Start by reviewing this book and ask yourself what your weakest areas are. By lasering in on weaknesses and then analyzing that specific area after each meeting, you can make rapid progress.

For many reps, an honest analysis of what they say and do in meetings will reveal bad habits, ones that are holding them back in almost every meeting. However, seeing our own shortcomings in the way we use words and in our body language is a real challenge, and in two ways.

For one, it is difficult to observe ourselves. Our verbal tics and body language under pressure are not obvious to us because we are inside them, and it just seems normal to us. For two, it is just plain painful to admit to ourselves that we are making the same mistakes over and over and that others are likely noticing it.

However, if you have the courage and honesty to face up to it, your performance in sales meetings can take a giant leap forward with "addition by subtraction."

I remember one rep who was on my team who had a habit of saying, "Youze guys" quite frequently in meetings. This was a common expression from his childhood, and it had nothing to do with his intelligence or abilities. It was just simply that he was used to saying it that way, and it came out in meetings. These were meetings where we were asking some of the biggest firms in the world for millions of dollars in business, and this ungrammatical expression was jarring.

To his credit, once he recognized what he was doing, he began to work immediately to cut it out. As with any habit we are correcting, there can be occasional slip-ups on the road to total elimination, but recognizing it is the first huge step on that path

In my experience, the overwhelming majority of reps don't even know if they have a performance issue, because they fail to do any self-examination. Nor do they seek out a coach, which is kind of ironic considering all their favorite athletes, writers, musicians, actors, politicians, entrepreneurs, etc., have likely sought out multiple coaches to become the tops in their industry. And they often are paired with a manager who does not know enough themselves to help.

Sometimes what is holding you back is not a verbal tic, but a matter of body language or unconscious bias. When I coached sales reps as a front-line manager, I developed a system of case studies (essentially role play on steroids with a real-world feel). In one of these specific exercises, the scenario was someone going into a meeting with many C-level executives. The rep entering the room didn't know everyone's title—that was part of the discovery exercise.

In the room, there were several vice presidents, all of them male. The only woman in the role play was the CEO. This rep entered this meeting and shook hands with everyone but the CEO! When this was pointed out to him after the exercise, he was distraught and did not understand how he made that mistake.

Was it a slip-up because of an unconscious bias, or maybe just a random mistake? Was it a fear of engaging directly with a CEO, the most powerful person in the room? Was it just a momentary brain malfunction? Some introspection may help answer that, but what really matters is exposing the mistake to yourself and then consciously correcting it.

In fact, that is really the whole point of all the reviewing and getting an objective look at yourself. You need to find ways to surface the mistakes you are committing and make them visible to yourself. That is half the battle. The other half is intentionally working to eliminate those things. It's an addition to your meeting skills simply by subtracting the bad stuff.

THOSE WHO ARE WILLING TO LEARN FROM OTHERS ARE THE ONES WHO ULTIMATELY WIN

By now, I have worked with a lot of sales reps, as a colleague, as their coach, and as their manager's leader. One of the surest signs of who will become good and who will ultimately fail is the attitude they bring to getting better and the passion they bring each day to do just that.

If they ignore feedback and think they will get by on charm, years served, or bluster, there is very little chance for success. The reps who ask a lot of questions and show that they truly hunger to get better are the ones who will become masters if they maintain their passion to be great at what they do. Interestingly enough, even the masters I've worked with continue to ask questions about their craft and performance. If you ever get to the point where you feel you can stop asking questions and no longer need to grow, that's not a good sign.

Passion is a necessary ingredient, but to actually improve, you have to know where to look for practical guidance so you can properly channel your enthusiasm for your craft. But where are the best places to turn?

Below are some of the "tried and true" ways to get objective feedback that takes you from amateur to true master.

Trusted Manager or Other Company Mentor

Anytime your manager or a more experienced salesperson joins you in a meeting, that is a golden opportunity to ask for honest feedback. This is working under the assumption that the person is truly engaged with what is going on in the meeting and understands the dynamics and context of the meeting you are in.

You may be in a situation where that is not the case, and your manager is either too busy or has the wrong personality to provide high-quality feedback. Are there other people (like a top rep, a leading sales engineer, another exec, etc.) within the company who you can tactfully and appropriately go to for meeting mentorship? I hope it is obvious that you will want any person you ask to be a mentor to be someone who has proven successful over the long term.

Record Yourself

Viewing yourself presenting at a meeting will be a gold mine of insight. Admittedly, this is not always easy to arrange for a live meeting, as it could turn into a distraction.

However, in some cases, your sales manager or trainer may set up practice meetings with your team. Recording these sessions can be eye-opening. Focus especially on the non-verbal signals, like the tone and energy you bring as you present.

Of course, you also have the option to record yourself at home when you are practicing your pitch. This is not the same as doing it live with the pressure of an audience, but it will give you a sense of self-presentation. It also can add to your confidence through the power of practice.

Please note that while video is better, sometimes audio is the only option to record at a live meeting. By all means, use this. Even without the visuals, you will be able to analyze verbal tics, how confident your voice is, your tone and naturalness, and a general sense of how well you are connecting with your audience.

Hire Coaches

Hiring coaches to level up your skills is one of the most overlooked ways to accelerate mastering your art or really any skill you want to get better at. I can testify to this personally because I have invested large amounts of time and money in all sorts of coaching, and it has been richly rewarding.

One particular coaching experience I remember was from my acting days. I hired Lesly Kahn & Co., a well-known acting coach, for auditions located in Los Angeles. This particular time I wanted help in improving my comedic timing for an upcoming audition for a big hit show on NBC Universal at the time.

What the coaching helped me with seemed incredibly small. It was what I took to be minor tweaks having to do with timing and delivery, and it did not feel all that earth-shattering.

Then I showed up for my audition, and it was one of the most amazing experiences in my acting life. The casting director and support staff could not stop laughing as each unique comedic beat landed. They had me repeat the scene three times, and each time the moments hit their mark and were met with uncontrollable laughter.

What made this even more remarkable is that, in general, casting folks train themselves to not react and are usually poker-faced about auditions. I would like to take credit as if I was some kind of natural comedic genius, but the truth is it was some simple and relatively small changes under the guidance of a coach for minor things I didn't even know I needed to work on.

I have found again and again in my sales career that coaching ups my game, and there is always something you can get a little better at.

This is an important thing to understand about hiring a coach—the part about aiming to get a *little* better. You can and should be surgical about hiring someone to get better at one specific skill. Focus on getting incrementally better and look to hire for specific skills.

It can be a trap to think that every coaching experience needs to have a profound massive impact or be a long relationship. Gaining incremental improvement on specific skills will eventually add up to big leaps forward, so never be afraid to hire a coach for a quick, focused engagement.

How should you choose a coach? It is important not to complicate this. Reviewing testimonials and checking out the experience level are two obvious ways to start. More importantly, most coaches put out free content online, whether it be blog posts, YouTube videos, or an email newsletter. Some will offer a free or low-cost quick consultation to measure whether you are a match.

Consume this content and ask yourself whether you sense a connection. If you do, and they have solid credentials and experience, pull the trigger. Since you will be someone who continually invests in coaching, some will have better outcomes than others. You will get something out of everything, even if one of the lessons is getting better at selecting coaches.

Where to Learn More About Movement and Voice Techniques

There are many movement and voice techniques that help an actor get into their body and become grounded to have stronger voices. You can also learn to have more control over your voice and how you present. These voice and movement skills are of tremendous benefit in sales, too. This work leads to becoming more present in the now and alive within your instrument (your voice/body). If you live in a major city, there will likely be an in-person class you can take.

Here are some recommended classes to do a search for in your area:

- Williamson Technique

- Feldenkraiss Technique

- Michael Chekov/Mask Work

- Viewpoints

- Modern Dance & Drum Circles

- Private voice coaches (for speaking and singing)

Teamwork

If you have a manager or team leader who runs role-playing scenarios or other team exercises, take these seriously because these can be invaluable "playgrounds" where you can fail and learn without it damaging any customer relationships.

If this is not happening in your company, consider teaming up with some of your fellow sales team members to practice pitches, entrances and exits, and give each other feedback.

Another alternative is to show your manager the elevated role-playing exercise I have on my website https://www.techsaleswarrior .com/ (mentioned previously in Chapter 5). On the site, you will find advice and a sample exercise for improving the training of the entire sales team in the art of meetings.

AS YOU ANALYZE, DON'T OVERLOOK THE OBVIOUS

A lot of what's been covered in this chapter is objective but is not precisely measurable. For instance, there isn't a percentage metric you can assign for how good your eye contact is in meetings. (Although there are newer softwares that attempt to perfect sales meetings by monitoring slides and attention, their guidance is extremely broad, and I don't find they help with precise direction. They are kind of like a bad director who says what is wrong but can't help you get it right outside of general notes.)

But there are completely objective stats that you can and should track carefully. Don't forget these. If you are working on getting better at meetings and you are not seeing gains over time in your closing percentages, you know there is still a lot of work to do.

Two stats you should be tracking:

1. Conversion rate from first meeting to trial or next meeting
2. Conversion rate from trial to purchase order

These are valuable meeting-related statistics, and if you are not seeing steady progress on improving these metrics over three months or six months (depending on your average sales cycle), you need to question why.

Another thing I hope is obvious to you: it is up to you to become your own judge and barometer of how you did in a meeting. As much as I have stressed getting outside perspectives in this chapter, ultimately, you need to train yourself to reflect often on your performance and ways to incrementally improve. Practice is the only way you will get better at this skill.

After every meeting, set aside some time as soon as you can for reflection. Think first about how you feel about your overall performance. Then get granular:

- How well did your questions expose problems and pain? How did you leverage the answers to drive the need for your solution in a calm, organic, and logical manner?
- How was the delivery of your pitch—did you have it down cold and adjust it to your customer?
- Did you check in for feedback often?
- Did you think like a good improv player, "Yes, and…"?
- What was your non-language communication—did your eye contact, body language, voice control, etc., send the right messages?
- Did you work to rid yourself of harmful tics and phrases?
- Thinking back on the meeting, how do you feel? How do you think each of the prospects in the meeting felt about it? What's one thing that could have been improved that you could have done?

It can be valuable to do this kind of analysis in a journaling exercise. Practice being brutally honest with yourself but without making it personal. Do not descend into beating yourself up with "I'm the worst" statements.

Instead, remind yourself of the mindset of being willing to fail along the road to becoming a master of the art of the sales meeting. I promise that if you truly commit to implementing the concepts in this book, the rewards will be enormous.

Action Steps for Chapter 10

- True masters are always on a relentless quest to get better at their craft. If you think you no longer have anything to learn or improve, you are falling into a mindset trap.

- Get practical help, including hiring coaches. Many times, the best use of a coach is to get granular and focus on one important skill. This is a great way to make progress.

- The more perspectives you can get when analyzing how you are doing, the better. Video, trusted colleagues, your own mirror—use anything that can reflect back to your areas to improve.

- Get in the habit of analyzing how you did after each meeting. For some meetings, this may just be a quick debrief with yourself. For more significant meetings, taking some time to journal about how you did is a great habit.

- The benefits of becoming a master of the art of the sales meeting are amazing. Do the work, and reap the rewards.

CONCLUSION

It was a meeting that had all the forebodings of turning into a nightmare scenario.

There were three of us headed to this meeting on a large national security-type campus. We lost some time getting our credentials checked and then more time trying to find the right building.

But we had planned ahead by building in a cushion of time, and we got there with time to spare.

We entered a room where a frazzled group of prospects waited for their boss to arrive. The room had all these tiny chairs that looked like they were built for grade schoolers. There was one bigger chair (a normal chair for an adult), but everyone else was in these small chairs. The sales engineer and I sat in two of these ridiculously small chairs ourselves. There was only one chair left—the big one—so the sales engineer trainee we had brought along sat in it.

Everyone seemed too nervous for the situation. I had known from some preliminary dealings with this prospective customer that the boss had a reputation for being intimidating and rough on both vendors and his own people, but the atmosphere in the room seemed extreme even for that.

Then in swaggered this guy, ten minutes late. No hello, and he immediately barked at the trainee sitting in the one normal-size seat that she had to move, and then promptly put himself in that place. It was an awkward and embarrassing scene to open. I gave up my chair and stood.

It was clear that everything was designed to elevate this guy's authority and make those around him less. Still, we were there for a reason, so I plunged ahead. I kicked things off by trying to go into discovery, asking questions about what problems they needed solved. He would have none of it.

"Just present what you are offering," was all he would give us. I proceeded to make the pitch. But he would abruptly chime in frequently, derailing what I was trying to share. There were a couple of moments when he challenged us in a dismissive, rude tone.

There was so much that felt outside our control in this meeting. He was surrounded by a scared team that wasn't going to stand up to him and tell him why our solution was the right fit and necessary. We were up against a grumpy decision-maker who did not seem interested in giving us a fair hearing. And he was ready to pounce on any sign of weakness on our part. There were moments where I considered ending the meeting completely and walking our team out in spite, but he walked right up to the line without going over it, so we proceeded.

It felt like long odds, but here is what we did.

First, I left my emotional judgment about his behavior to the side. I came to accomplish a goal, not to decide whether someone's behavior was acceptable or not. If he had gone to the point of completely offending my sales engineer and the trainee, we would have walked. But we let him feel tough to win the upper hand for this meeting. Maybe he had had terrible experiences with incompetent sales reps wasting his time in the past. Maybe he had a terrible childhood. Maybe he was just a mean son of a gun and always would be. But for what we needed to complete our mission, those judgments were irrelevant.

Second, I mirrored him. By this, I, of course, do not mean I became rude and dismissive myself. But I did take a "stand my ground" attitude, matching his no-nonsense posture and strong voice with very direct numbers and stats that were defensible.

Third, I relied on my preparation and research. I knew from his team that they had a real problem with data security, that it was serious, and that the product I was selling could solve it. I laid out an airtight case in a logical and technical way of exactly what the problems were and how our solution could resolve them.

It was almost like he was a skeptical juror, and my partner and I put together an airtight case that convinced him that he and his team had a serious problem beyond a reasonable doubt. And that there was also no doubt we knew our stuff and could fix it. I usually wait to shift to this more commanding persona later in a sales cycle, but there was no time or empathy with this individual, so we had to get to the proofs now.

By the end of the meeting, he was much more engaged and in a more productive way. While no one would have confused him with Mother Teresa at any point, we had clearly turned him from an angry skeptic to someone open to a real solution.

We eventually earned the business, and in a later communication, he said it was "the best meeting I ever had."

WHY BECOMING A MASTER OF THE ART OF THE SALES MEETING IS WORTH IT

Becoming a master of meetings is good for your bank account because you will close more customers. But that's not really the deepest benefit of mastery.

The real benefit is knowing you can handle any scenario, even potentially nightmarish ones, with confidence and skill. And that you can meet with every title under the sun with ease. You still may go into some meetings with fear, but you will know how to use that and transform it into excitement.

If I had one wish for all the readers of this book, it would be that you could go into a meeting like I just described above and handle it like a total pro, with confidence, passion, and fun. I promise you it is possible; you just have to work hard and keep improving, through both failure and success.

This brings to mind some words that the gifted actor Bryan Cranston shared several years ago:

The best advice for fellow actors is this: know what your job is. About eighteen years ago, I had this cognition that I realized I was going into auditions trying to get a job. And that simply wasn't what I was doing; it wasn't what I'm supposed to be doing. An actor is supposed to create a compelling, interesting character that serves the text. You present it in the environment where your audition happens. And then you walk away. And that's it. Everything else is out of your control. So don't even think of it, don't focus on that. You're not going there to get a job. You're going there to present what you do. You act. And there it is. And walk away. And there's power in that. And there's confidence in that.[10]

I think we need to think like this in complex enterprise sales. The focus should not be on some abstract idea of "just get the sale" (in the same way Cranston decided to stop trying to "get a job"). We cannot go into a room desperately thinking, "Somehow, someway, I need the PO."

We need to focus on what is in front of us. Uncover pain and align on value. Bring insights on what we have done for other firms similar to the situation we are in now. Demonstrate with clarity how we can solve the problem at hand, and then let it lead us to the next steps. Be present and do what is in front of us. Know what your mission is at the moment and control what you can

---

[10] Oscars, "Bryan Cranston's Advice to Actors," YouTube video, 1:22, September 27, 2013, https://www.youtube.com/watch?v=v1WiCGq-PcY.

control, and then take action. And then walk out knowing you did your best.

As Cranston said: "There's power in that."

Yes, you will inevitably lose some sales; there are always factors outside your control. But that will not take away from your confidence because you know that a healthy portion of leads will get across the finish line because you are consistently doing the right things in meetings. And for the ones that don't close, there's always a lesson to be learned to get better in the process.

FOCUS ON THIS

I hope this book has fired you up to get better at your performance and craft and you realize the power that is within you. The words you say, how you say them, the passion you bring to your work, and your presence all have dramatic effects on your overall success in sales. Here is what I want to leave you with as you begin the journey toward meeting mastery.

- With discipline and focus, you can get better at all types of meetings and increase your conversion rates.
- Making the most of every "meeting" is predominantly in your control and depends on how well you have prepared for it.
- Becoming a better listener and more effective speaker greatly increases your impact in any room.

- The art of a meeting is usually decisive on whether a prospect chooses to do business with you or not. Your preparation, speech, dress, ability to listen, pace a meeting, and economical responses will all come into play. Yet these factors are too little focused on in most meeting training.
- Leveraging the craft of performance, you can identify ways to improve your skills (voice, body language, ability to hear and respond to pain) in a way that makes you more effective and efficient.
- What isn't inspected isn't improved. Sales, like life, is a journey. The more you practice technical skills and develop your art, the better you will get. This is why consistently analyzing your performance through self-assessment, coaching, and feedback is so important.

Finally, remember that it is always about focusing on solving problems and relieving pain for your customers. Go into each meeting with a goal that moves you closer to doing just that, and you will become a true master of the art of the sales meeting.

FINALE

Many years ago, I had the honor of auditioning for a role on the Warner Brothers' lot, the legendary site where so many great movies have been filmed. It was for the lead in a new series of big-budget movies about Superman. As things shook out, Henry Cavill would become the new Superman in *Man of Steel*, and then would go on to play him for many of the sequels.

Despite not getting the role, being in a position to legitimately compete for a huge role on a fabled movie lot was a validation of what so many of my coaches had taught me up to that point: With great focus, small steps in the right direction, and consistent daily discipline, you will fly to heights you never imagined.

As I write this now, it has been just over a decade from the time of that audition. My sales career journey pulled me back east to New York City and then to Washington, DC, but now I am back in Los Angeles, living about a stone's throw from that same Warner Brothers' lot.

Of course, no one is buying a ticket to view my sales results or see the growth of my team. But you will not catch me complaining. Quite the opposite. I have been incredibly blessed, gratified, and humbled by where my journey in sales has taken me. It has felt like something that has come full circle, both in my training and geographically. The acting training laid the foundation for success in sales, and it also has brought me back to live in the land of movie magic.

In both this book and my previous one, I have emphasized that sales is not some kind of sleazy enterprise where the object is to fool the customer into buying. That is a false and damaging stereotype that no young salesperson should believe. The best salespeople are those who truly care about helping others and want everyone to win in a deal. You can feel true satisfaction in your sales career, and no ticket-buying audience or applause is necessary. There is plenty of magic and excitement in helping people solve problems and getting rewarded beyond your wildest dreams for it.

My hope is that you are inspired to go on your own journey, a never-ending quest to get better at your craft, and to know the confidence and empowerment that comes from succeeding in tech sales.

Now—go turn those dreams into action.

ACKNOWLEDGMENTS

Time to roll the credits…

Throughout my life, I've had countless coaches and teachers who have guided me, challenged me, and pushed me to new horizons in business, spirituality, performing, writing, physical conditioning, sports, service, relationships, travel, critical thinking, movement, family, finances, and the game of life. You helped shape me into who I have become, and I owe much of that to you. Thank You! I'll never forget the dedication and time you invested in me.

For all the coaches, teachers, and leaders out there who fight through resistance to help sharpen skills and create new possibilities. Thank you, keep up the great work!

For my Varonis team, new and old, thank you for the honor of working together, innovating, implementing, and building upon this notable work to be better each day.

For Lauren Celinski for cheering me on with the many hours of work it takes to pursue writing and to complete a manuscript outside of leading and growing a big team of sellers. You are an amazing partner and friend!

For all my family and friends for the inspiration, ongoing support, and motivation to climb higher. You push me to keep growing and keep serving in new ways!

A special thanks to everyone at Scribe for helping me dive deeper and complete our second book together. I want to especially thank David Moffitt at Scribe for fine-tuning the material every step of the way over the last year together—you've been an awesome partner in this writing journey, two times over now! Thanks to Sophie May for keeping us on track, Marietta Anastassatos for delivering a beautiful cover nearly identical on paper to a vision in my head, Skyler Gray for another assist with building the perfect title, Kelly Teemer for amazing support in PR and marketing, Laura Cail and Christian Dufner for proofreading, and the rest of the Scribe team who helped bring this to life.

Thank you to the awesome Dana Patrick for the author photo.

For the creative artists, who take on all the risk while pursuing and growing in their talents, you're an inspiration. Keep up the good fight!

For my readers, thanks for supporting my books and sharing the messages with your teams. I hope they are as impactful as intended. I greatly appreciate your Amazon reviews in advance! They help spread the word. Email me below with any cool stories or how the work has impacted you. Would love to hear from you. Thank You!

And for all of you brave, courageous sellers out there who seek to do the good work and get better in the process every single day —thank you for your commitment! Seeing you grow in your craft while crushing quota consistently and positively impacting more lives around you as a result of your success has been one of the greatest joys in my career.

"Great oaks from little acorns grow."

—14TH CENTURY PROVERB

See you in the field!

Readers: Let me know how the journey is going. If this book helped you at all, send me a note; I'd love to hear about how you are implementing it. For questions or comments, email me at techsaleswarrior@gmail.com. For networking or if interested in products or services, connect with me on LinkedIn at linkedin.com /in/chrisprangley. You can also visit my website: www.techsales warrior.com.

ABOUT THE AUTHOR

CHRIS PRANGLEY is the Vice President of Sales-West for a multibillion-dollar cybersecurity firm and the author of *The Tech Sales Warrior*. With more than a decade of sales experience in the enterprise B2B market, Chris helps global firms solve challenges in data security, collaboration, threat detection, and governance. He has a proven track record of overachieving customer expectations while building successful sales teams known for cultivating strong relationships and surpassing quotas. He graduated from Loyola University Chicago with a BBA in marketing and a minor in philosophy. A former actor and frequent speaker, Chris studied the craft of performance extensively with leading coaches from NYU, Yale, UCLA, the Groundlings, Upright Citizens Brigade, and the William Esper Studio.

Made in the USA
Las Vegas, NV
20 January 2024

84643379R00142